Mathematics
FOR COMMON ENTRANCE

13+
LEVEL 3

Exam Practice Answers

Mathematics

FOR COMMON ENTRANCE

13+ LEVEL 3

Exam Practice Answers

David E. Hanson

GALORE PARK

AN HACHETTE UK COMPANY

About the author

David Hanson has over 40 years' experience of teaching and has been Leader of the ISEB 11+ Maths setting team and a member of the ISEB Editorial Endorsement Committee. He has also edited the SATIPS Maths Broadsheet. David has retired from teaching to run a small shop trading in collectors' items.

Acknowledgements

I would like to thank Gina de Cova for her assistance at the early stages of this publication.

David Hanson, July 2016

Every effort has been made to trace all copyright holders, but if any have been inadvertently overlooked, the Publishers will be pleased to make the necessary arrangements at the first opportunity.

Although every effort has been made to ensure that website addresses are correct at time of going to press, Galore Park cannot be held responsible for the content of any website mentioned in this book. It is sometimes possible to find a relocated web page by typing in the address of the home page for a website in the URL window of your browser.

Hachette UK's policy is to use papers that are natural, renewable and recyclable products and made from wood grown in sustainable forests. The logging and manufacturing processes are expected to conform to the environmental regulations of the country of origin.

Orders: please contact Bookpoint Ltd, 130 Park Drive, Milton Park, Abingdon, Oxon OX14 4SE. Telephone: (44) 01235 827720. Fax: (44) 01235 400454. Email education@bookpoint.co.uk Lines are open from 9 a.m. to 5 p.m., Monday to Saturday, with a 24-hour message answering service. Visit our website at www.galorepark.co.uk for details of other revision guides for Common Entrance, examination papers and Galore Park publications.

ISBN: 978 1 4718 6893 1

© David Hanson 2016

First published in 2016 by

Galore Park Publishing Ltd

An Hachette UK Company

Carmelite House

50 Victoria Embankment

London EC4Y 0DZ

www.galorepark.co.uk

Impression number   10 9 8 7 6 5 4 3 2 1

Year   2020 2019 2018 2017 2016

Illustrations by Aptara, Inc.

Typeset in India

Printed in the UK

A catalogue record for this title is available from the British Library.

Contents

Introduction

This book includes all answers for the questions in *Mathematics for Common Entrance 13+ Exam Practice Questions Level 3*.

The curriculum and the examination syllabus

The mathematics curriculum and the examination syllabus are subject to relatively minor changes or different emphases from time to time, whereas the body of mathematical skills and knowledge which teachers consider valuable seems to remain fairly constant.

For completeness, and to allow greater flexibility in the use of this material, some questions included in *Exam Practice Questions Level 3* may be outside the syllabus currently examined, even though they are likely to be within the capability of the majority of students in most schools. It is left to teachers to select questions which they consider appropriate and it is assumed that teachers will wish to differentiate according to student abilities.

The material is appropriate for KS3 studies but, for completeness, questions cover ideas met in all years up to Year 8.

The contents pages outline the way in which questions have been grouped in six 'strands': Number; Calculations; Solving problems; Algebra; Geometry and measures; Statistics and probability. The sections within the strands have been numbered for easier reference.

Examination levels

Level 1 and Level 2 papers are based upon the same syllabus, but some of the questions in Level 1 papers will be generally more accessible.

Many of the questions in *Exam Practice Questions Level 3* will be accessible to all students and it is assumed that teachers and parents will wish to encourage students to attempt questions that may be just beyond the requirements for the intended examination.

It is expected that the majority of students will take Level 2 papers.

Questions that are more demanding and may be more appropriate for candidates taking papers at Level 2 and above are indicated by a Level 2 symbol in the *Exam Practice Questions* book. Level 3 and CASE papers are based upon the extended syllabus, and questions appropriate for Level 3 and CASE candidates are indicated by a Level 3 symbol in *Exam Practice Questions*. The level indicators are not printed in this answers book.

The level notes are included as a guide only and most of the questions are suitable for students taking papers at any level.

It is strongly recommended that reference is made regularly to the current examination syllabus and to recent past papers.

Using *Mathematics for Common Entrance 13+ Exam Practice Questions Level 3*

The book has been designed for use by students, under the guidance of a teacher or parent, as a resource for practice of basic skills and recall of knowledge.

It is assumed that, in addition to plain paper, the following grids will be available for use where appropriate:

● centimetre squared

● centimetre square dotted

- centimetre isometric dotted
- graph (cm and 2 mm).

If students are permitted to draw in the *Exam Practice Questions* book, then valuable time may be saved.
Students are expected to

- show full working where appropriate and, at all times, to make their method clear to the marker
- produce a personal record of achievement which will prove valuable as an additional revision aid.

It is assumed that, throughout, students will

- make use of estimation skills
- pay attention to the order of operations (BIDMAS or BODMAS)
- use strategies to check the reasonableness of results
- use a calculator only when instructed or allowed to do so.

Whilst this book has been compiled for use in independent schools, it is expected that it will also prove useful for students in state schools and home schoolers.

The questions

Questions follow the ISEB format and are numbered either:

1 (a)

(b)

(c) where parts of questions are not related.

or

1 (i)

(ii)

(iii) where parts of questions are related.

Almost all of the questions are modelled on questions from past Common Entrance 13+ papers, using similar wording and mark allocation.

Within each broad group of questions, some grading in difficulty has been attempted and harder questions may be found towards the end of each grouping. Many of these harder questions will be within the capabilities of most students.

Many questions involve several skills. These questions have been placed wherever seemed most appropriate.

The number of questions on a particular topic reflects the frequency with which such questions have appeared in the Common Entrance papers.

Using *Mathematics for Common Entrance 13+ Exam Practice Answers Level 3*

It is hoped that students will be permitted to write and draw in their copies of the *Exam Practice Questions* book, since this will save time, especially with graphical work, and also make marking more straightforward.

Teachers and parents will decide on the way that they wish students to present their work for marking.

In questions where stages of working and/or explanations are expected, credit should be given for evidence of appropriate reasoning. Where drawings are involved, it is suggested that evidence of understanding is more important than accuracy.

Calculators

Questions in 1.1, 1.2, 2.1 and 2.2 should be tackled without a calculator.
In 3.1, 4.2, 5.2 and 6.1 a calculator should not be needed.
Questions in 2.3 require the use of a suitable calculator.
Questions which involve both calculator and non-calculator parts have the parts clearly indicated.
It is assumed that students will

- be encouraged to tackle all other questions without the use of a calculator

- have the opportunity to decide for themselves when the use of a calculator is appropriate and when other methods are more effective.

Final preparations for the exam

Familiarity with a selection of recent past papers of the appropriate level will remind students of what can be expected.
Students at any level will sit three papers:

- a non-calculator paper of the appropriate level

- a calculator paper of the appropriate level

- a mental arithmetic test which is common to all three levels.

Tips on taking the exam

Before the exam students should

- get all their equipment ready the night before. They will need: calculator, pens, pencils, rubber, pencil sharpener, ruler, protractor, compasses, set square.

- make sure they are at their best by getting a good night's sleep before the exam.

- have a good breakfast in the morning.

- take some water into the exam if this is allowed.

- think positively and keep calm.

1 Number

→ **1.1 Properties of numbers**

1	**(a)**	(1), 2, 3, 6, 7, 14, 21, (42)	(1)	**(e)**	16		(1)
	(b)	3 or 5	(1)	**(f)**	2		(1)
	(c)	example 48, 72, 96	(1)	**(g)**	125		(1)
	(d)	53 or 59	(1)	**(h)**	2		(1)
2	**(i)**	36	(1)	**(iv)**	47		(1)
	(ii)	4	(1)	**(v)**	18		(1)
	(iii)	39	(1)				
3	**(i)**	9	(2)				
	(ii)	$^-$5 and 5 or $^-$2 and 2	(1)				
	(iii)	$^-$5 and 8	(2)				
	(iv)	**(a)** $6 + {}^-5 = 1$	(1)	**(c)**	$^-1 \times {}^-4 = 4$		(2)
		(b) $5 - {}^-2 = 7$	(1)	**(d)**	$8 \div 2 = 4$		(2)
4	**(a)**	**(i)** 3	(1)	**(iii)**	11		(1)
		(ii) 2	(1)	**(iv)**	7		(2)
	(b)	**(i)** $^-$12	(1)	**(iii)**	$^-$8		(1)
		(ii) 30	(1)	**(iv)**	$^-$3		(1)
5	**(i)**	**(a)** 66	(2)	**(b)**	102		(2)
	(ii)	36	(1)				
6	**(a)**	**(i)** 72	(2)	**(b)**	$2^2 \times 5 \times 11$		(3)
		(ii) 10	(1)				
7	**(a)**	990					(2)
	(b)	$2 \times 5 \times 23$					(3)
	(c)	484 ($2^2 \times 11^2$)					(2)
	(d)	5 and 37, 11 and 31, 13 and 29, 19 and 23					(2)
8	**(a)**	17.8, 17.58, 17.5, 17.35	(2)	**(d)**	1188		(2)
	(b)	17	(2)	**(e)**	83 and 89		(3)
	(c)	$5^2 \times 17$	(3)				
9	**(i)**	$2^2 \times 3 \times 5 \times 7$	(3)	**(ii)**	60 ($2^2 \times 3 \times 5$)		(2)

10	(a)	25	(1)	(c)	Examples 3 and 17, 5 and 19	(1)
	(b)	$\frac{25}{27}$	(2)	(d)	$2^4 \times 5^2$	(3)

11   0.22, $\frac{1}{4}$, 26%, $\frac{3}{10}$ (3)

12	(a)	(i)	550	(1)	(iii)	48	(1)
		(ii)	1000	(1)			
	(b)	(i)	30.7	(1)	(iii)	210	(1)
		(ii)	0.41	(1)	(iv)	0.0510	(2)

13	(a)	(i)	36	(1)	(ii)	8	(2)
	(b)	(i)	100	(1)	(ii)	30	(2)

14   0.6, $\frac{5}{9}$, $\frac{27}{50}$, 53%   (4)

15   100   (3)

16	(a)	2	(3)			
	(b)	(i)	3864.5	(1)	(ii)	131	(2)
	(c)	2.739	(2)			

17	(a)	(i)	XLIII	(1)	(iii)	MMMXVI	(1)
		(ii)	CCCLXXIX	(1)	(iv)	CMXCIX	(1)
	(b)	(i)	24	(1)	(iii)	1666	(1)
		(ii)	555	(1)	(iv)	2777	(1)

18	(a)	(i)	5.3×10^4	(1)	(ii)	8.9×10^{-3}	(1)
	(b)	(i)	130 000 000	(1)	(ii)	0.0705	(1)

19	(a)	3×10^9	(2)	(b)	$3 : 1 000 000$	(3)

→ 1.2 Fractions, decimals, percentages; ratio

1	(a)	(i)	$\frac{5}{9}$	(1)	(ii)	$\frac{5}{12}$	(2)
	(b)	(i)	$\frac{32}{40}$	(1)	(iii)	80%	(1)
		(ii)	0.8	(1)			

2	(a)	$\frac{4}{9}$	(1)			
	(b)	(i)	1	(1)	(ii)	$\frac{13}{4}$	(1)
	(c)	(i)	4.6	(2)	(ii)	85%	(2)

3

Fraction (in lowest terms)	Decimal	Percentage
$\frac{2}{5}$	0.4	40%
$\frac{6}{25}$	0.24	24%
$\frac{7}{20}$	0.35	35%

(6)

4 (a) Examples $\frac{4}{6}$, $\frac{6}{9}$ (2)   (b) 181.8 cm   (3)

5 (a) $\frac{12}{25}$ (2)   (c) 62.5%   (2)

   (b) $\frac{9}{20}$ (2)

6 (a) $\frac{3}{20}$ (2)   (c) £140   (2)

   (b) 0.52   (2)   (d) 5.2 km   (2)

7 (a) (i) £3.60   (2)   (ii) £9.10   (2)

   (b) 5%   (2)

8 (a) (i) 12%   (2)   (ii) $\frac{22}{25}$ (2)

   (b) (i) Jacket A (A costs £34; B costs £36)   (2)

      (ii) £16   (2)

9 (a) 39 cases of 'flu   (2)

   (b) (i) 180 kg   (1)   (ii) 162 kg   (1)

10 (i) (a) £80   (2)   (ii) £456   (3)

    (b) £480   (1)

11 (i) £116   (2)

   (ii) (a) £174   (1)   (b) 150%   (2)

12 (i) $\frac{1}{2}$ (3)   (ii) $\frac{1}{6}$ (2)

13 (a) $\frac{4}{9}$ (1)

   (b) (i) $\frac{2}{3}$ shaded   (1)

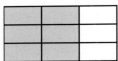

      (ii) $\frac{1}{3}$ (2)

14 (a) $\frac{17}{20}$ (2)

   (b) (i) $\frac{2}{5}$ (2)   (ii) $\frac{1}{5}$ (2)

15 (a) $2\frac{1}{30}$ (2) (c) $7\frac{1}{2}$ (2)

   (b) $2\frac{1}{6}$ (2)

16 (a) $\frac{11}{15}$ (2) (c) $\frac{3}{4}$ (2)

   (b) $1\frac{1}{6}$ (2) (d) $2\frac{4}{5}$ (2)

17 (a) $3\frac{7}{12}$ (3) (b) $2\frac{1}{4}$ (3)

18 (a) $2\frac{7}{20}$ (3) (b) $1\frac{21}{44}$ (3)

19 (a) £27 (2)

   (b) (i) £22.50 (2)

       (ii) Takings rose by 27 pence.

           He sold 23 (0.92 × 25) burgers at 99p (1.1 × 90p) each, taking £22.77 (4)

20 (i) 7 : 15 (1) (ii) 7 : 8 (1)

21 (i) 1 : 4 (3 : 12) (1) (iii) 5 : 3 (1)

   (ii) 4 : 5 (1)

22 (a) (i) 105 (2) (ii) 104 (2)

   (b) 10 cm (3)

23 (a) £68 (2) (b) 270 g (2)

24 (i) 2 : 5 (2) (iii) $\frac{3}{19}$ (3)

   (ii) 80 (2)

25 (i) (a) 14% (1) (b) 12.5% (2)

   (ii) 10 cm (2)

26 (i) (a) $1\frac{9}{16}$ (3) (b) $12\frac{1}{12}$ (3)

   (ii) $10\frac{25}{48}$ (3)

27 (i) 6 (1) (iii) $8\frac{15}{16}$ (3)

   (ii) $\frac{1}{2}$ (2) (iv) $1\frac{2}{11}$ (4)

28 (i) $11\frac{7}{16}$ pounds (2) (ii) $3\frac{13}{16}$ pounds (3)

29 (i) $48\frac{1}{8}$ m³ (3) (ii) $83\frac{1}{2}$ m² (5)

30 (i) $\frac{3}{4}$ (2) (iii) $1\frac{1}{8}$ (2)

   (ii) $\frac{1}{2}$ (1)

31 **(i)** **(a)** $\dfrac{1}{3}$ (1) **(b)** $\dfrac{1}{6} \dfrac{1}{(3 \times 2 \times 1)}$ (1)

(ii) $\dfrac{1}{24} \dfrac{1}{(4 \times 3 \times 2 \times 1)}$ (3)

(iii) Yes, it is probable that Belinda's idea will make money!

$\dfrac{1}{5040} \dfrac{1}{(7 \times 6 \times 5 \times 4 \times 3 \times 2 \times 1)}$

5040 × 10p entry charges would bring in £504, with the probability that there would be only one payout of £50 (3)

(iv) Barbara's name has the same number of letters but there are 2 Bs, 3 As and 2 Rs so the probability of picking out a B first is $\dfrac{2}{7}$ not $\dfrac{1}{7}$, and so on.

Barbara could not expect to have the same success as Belinda! (2)

5

2 Calculations

→ 2.1 Mental strategies

1 (a) £59.95   (1)   (d) £32   (1)
   (b) 2000   (1)   (e) 40 pence   (1)
   (c) 64   (1)

2 (a) £618   (1)   (d) £37   (1)
   (b) 1.25 km   (1)   (e) order 2   (1)
   (c) $\frac{7}{10}$ (70%)   (1)

3 (a) 237   (1)   (d) 240   (1)
   (b) £12   (1)   (e) 08:30   (1)
   (c) £63.75   (1)

4 (a) 36 900   (1)   (d) 32 cm (same as the original
   (b) 16 g   (1)   rectangle!)   (1)
   (c) 300 m   (1)   (e) 64 tiles   (1)

5 (a) 61   (1)   (d) 180 g   (1)
   (b) £210   (1)   (e) 115°   (1)
   (c) 79   (1)

6 (a) $\frac{3}{5}$ (1)   (d) 22 pages   (1)
   (b) £7   (1)   (e) £6.80   (1)
   (c) 3550   (1)

7 (a) 94   (1)   (d) 24 pence   (1)
   (b) 27 sweets   (1)   (e) 30   (1)
   (c) 40 023   (1)

8 (a) $\frac{4}{7}$ (1)   (d) £1.50   (1)
   (b) £22.10   (1)   (e) ⁻2 (negative two)   (1)
   (c) 6   (1)

9 (a) 28   (1)   (d) £230   (1)
   (b) 1.7   (1)   (e) 50 kg   (1)
   (c) 492   (1)

10 (a) £49 (1)   (d) 12 (1)
   (b) 3 (1)   (e) 300 (1)
   (c) $\frac{1}{5}$ (1)

11 (a) £2.61 (1)   (d) 11 (1)
   (b) 9 (1)   (e) 26 (1)
   (c) 64 (1)

12 (a) 470 cm (1)
   (b) ⁻7° Celsius (1)
   (c) 24 (1)
   (d) (1)

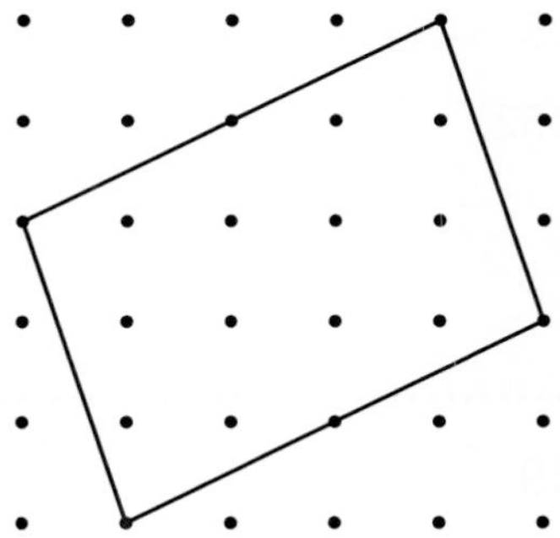

   (e) About 75 cm (1)

13 (a) LVIII (1)   (d) 4000 (1)
   (b) 10 (1)   (e) $\frac{1}{24}$ (1)
   (c) 20 (1)

14 (a) 40 cm² (1)   (d) 1000 (10³) (1)
   (b) 2.2 inches (1)   (e) 9.5 (1)
   (c) 70 g (1)

→ 2.2 Written methods

It is expected that working is clearly set out.

1 (a) 16.65 (2)   (c) 285.6 (2)
   (b) 5.72 (2)   (d) 10.35 (2)
2 (a) 7.73 (2)   (c) 23.75 (2)
   (b) 1.77 (2)   (d) 0.95 (2)
3 (a) 10.07 (2)   (c) 176.4 (2)
   (b) 4.89 (2)   (d) 3.6 (2)
4 (a) 7.98 (1)   (c) 14.732 (3)
   (b) 2.18 (2)   (d) 1.27 (2)

5	(a)	£14.50	(2)		(c)	£34.80	(2)
	(b)	£2.90	(2)		(d)	£1.45	(2)
6	(a)	27	(1)		(b)	53	(3)
7	(a)	(i) 166.6	(2)		(ii)	1.666	(1)
	(b)	(i) 3.4	(2)		(ii)	340	(2)
8	(a)	(i) 2383 g	(2)		(ii)	2.383 kg	(1)
	(b)	(i) 41.5 cm	(2)		(ii)	0.415 m	(1)
9	(a)	£471.20	(3)		(b)	£7.80	(3)
10	(a)	120.26	(2)		(c)	0.6624	(2)
	(b)	98.52	(2)		(d)	11.5	(2)
11	(a)	92.97	(1)		(c)	2.352	(2)
	(b)	60.3	(1)		(d)	7	(2)

→ 2.3 Calculator methods

1	(i)	10.50	(1)		(iii)	7.19	(2)
	(ii)	10	(2)				
2	(i)	(a) $\frac{60}{5\times 8}$	(2)		(b)	1.5	(1)
	(ii)	(a) 1.484 001 008	(2)		(c)	1.484	(1)
		(b) 1.48	(1)				
3	(i)	(a) £0.41 (41p)	(1)		(b)	£0.46 (46p)	(2)
	(ii)	£0.43 (43p)	(2)				
4	(i)	1806.79	(2)		(ii)	1800	(1)
5	(i)	1.537 313 433	(2)		(iii)	1.537	(1)
	(ii)	1.54	(1)				
6	(i)	16.689 872 83	(2)				
	(ii)	(a) 16.690	(1)		(b)	20	(1)
7	(a)	(i) 2931.461 458					(2)
		(ii) 2931.5					(1)
		(iii) 3000					(1)
	(b)	$\frac{800\times 0.2}{10\times 8} = 2$					(3)
8	(a)	(i) 198.8	(2)		(ii)	200	(1)
	(b)	20	(2)				
	(c)	(i) 2.086 254 782	(2)				
		(ii) 2.1	(1)				

Solving problems

→ 3.1 Reasoning about numbers or shapes

1 (i) $n - 1, n - 2$ (2)

(ii) $3n - 3 = 54 \rightarrow 3n = 57 \rightarrow n = 19$ (3)

(iii) 17 (1)

2 360 (the four scores must be 6, 5, 4 and 3) (4)

3 (i) 32 cm² (4) (ii) 88 cm² (2)

4 (i) (3)

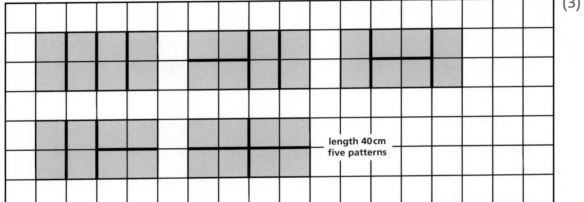

length 40 cm
five patterns

(ii) (4)

length 50 cm
eight patterns

(iii)

Length of pattern	Number of possible patterns
10 cm	1
20 cm	2
30 cm	3
40 cm	5
50 cm	8
60 cm	13

(4)

5 **(a)** **(i)** 60° (1)   **(iii)** 720° (1)

      (ii) 120° (1)

   (b) $16y = 720° \rightarrow y = 45°$ (4)

6 **(i)** **(a)** 12 (1)   **(b)** $h - 5$ (2)

   (ii) **(a)** 9 (1)

        (b) $h - 8$ (1)

        (c) $h - 8 + 9 \rightarrow h + 1$ (2)

   (iii) $h = 13$ (2)

7 **(i)** **(a)** 54 (1)   **(b)** 91 (2)

   (ii) 33 (3)

8 **(i)** 24 (2)   **(iii)** 4 : 3 (2)

   (ii) 13.5 (2)

9 **(i)** **(a)** 2997 (1)   **(b)** 0.002 997 002 997 … (2)

   (ii) **(a)** 6993 (1)   **(b)** 0.006 993 006 993 … (2)

   (iii) **(a)** First and second digits always zero (1)

        (b) Third digit one less than numerator of fraction (1)

        (c) Fourth digit always 9 (1)

        (d) Fifth digit always 9 (1)

        (e) Sixth digit always 10 minus numerator of fraction (or sixth digit always 9 minus third digit) (1)

   (iv) **(a)** $n - 1$ (2)

        (b) $10 - n$ (2)

10 **(i)** (5)

$3^2 - 0^2 =$	$9 - 0 = 9$	(3×3)
$4^2 - 1^2 =$	$16 - 1 = 15$	(3×5)
$5^2 - 2^2 =$	$25 - 4 = 21$	(3×7)
$6^2 - 3^2 =$	$36 - 9 = 27$	(3×9)
$7^2 - 4^2 =$	$49 - 16 = 33$	(3×11)
$8^2 - 5^2 =$	$64 - 25 = 39$	(3×13)
$9^2 - 6^2 =$	$81 - 36 = 45$	(3×15)

   (ii) All multiples of 3 (2)

   (iii) $3 \times 197 \rightarrow 591$ (for $a^2 - b^2$ in the left column, we have $3(a + b)$ in the right column) (3)

11 **(i)** 125, 230, 423   (3)

    (ii) **(a)** 13   (1)   **(c)** 4   (1)

          (b) 9   (1)

    (iii) Answers vary; example:

         A = 68, B = 125, C = 230, D = 423

         (a) 491   (1)   **(c)** 136   (1)

         (b) 355   (1)

    (iv) A = a, B = b, C = c, D = d

         (a) D is $a + b + c$ (1)   **(c)** B + C is $b + c$ (1)

         (b) A + D is $2a + b + c$ (1)   **(d)** (A + D) − (B + C) is $2a$ (1)

         (e) Answers vary; example: In (ii)(c) and (iii)(c) the answer is twice the value of A for the group of four terms A, B, C, D. For any group of four consecutive terms A, B, C, D of the sequence, the value of (A + D) − (B + C) is always twice the first term (2A).   (2)

12 **(i)** **(a)** x^2 (1)   **(b)** $\frac{x}{4}$ (1)

    (ii) $x^2 \div \frac{x}{4} = 64 \rightarrow \frac{4x}{1} = 64 \rightarrow 4x = 64 \rightarrow x = 16$ (3)

13 **(i)** 899   (1)

    (ii) 23 and 37 (23 × 37 = 851)   (3)

14 **(i)** **(a)** Even   (1)   **(c)** Even   (1)

         (b) Even   (1)

    (ii) **(a)** Odd   (1)   **(b)** Even   (1)

    (iii) Even   (1)

    (iv) $x = 8$, $y = 6$, $z = 3$ (3)

15 **(i)** Shapes with area 16 cm^2

    (a) Parallelogram   (1)   **(c)** Isosceles triangle   (2)

    (b) Kite   (2)

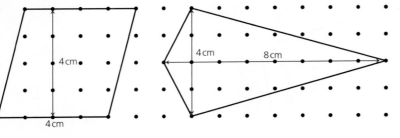

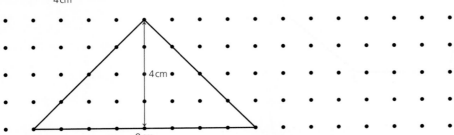

(ii) Shapes with perimeter 16 cm

    (a)   Rectangle   (1)   **(c)**   Isosceles triangle   (3)

    (b)   Parallelogram   (3)

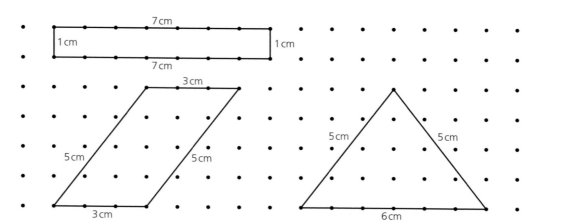

16 **(i)**   (2)

    (ii)   (2)

(iii) (2)

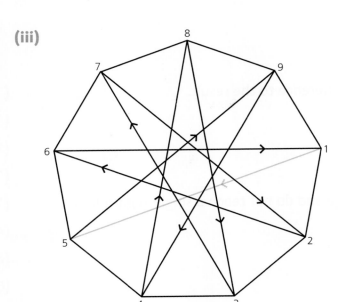

(iv) (a) (2)

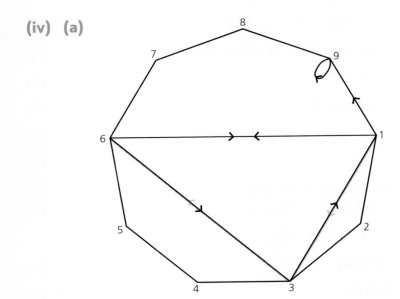

(b) 1 3 6 1 6 **3** **1** 9 9 (4)

Boy 9 eventually throws the ball to himself!

17 (i) (a) $48 \rightarrow 24 \rightarrow 12 \rightarrow 6$ (1)

(b) $45 \rightarrow 46 \rightarrow 23 \rightarrow 24 \rightarrow 12 \rightarrow 6$ (1)

(ii) (a) Double each time (1)

(b) Multiply by 2 and then subtract 1 (2)

(iii) $a = 145$, $b = 160$, $c = 16$ (3)

(iv) Answers vary; example:

$150 \rightarrow 75 \rightarrow 76 \rightarrow 38 \rightarrow 19 \rightarrow 20 \rightarrow 10 \rightarrow 5$ (3)

18 (i) (a) $53 \rightarrow 23 \rightarrow 11 \rightarrow 3$ (1)

(b) $81 \rightarrow 17 \rightarrow 15 \rightarrow 11 \rightarrow 3$ (1)

(c) $76 \rightarrow 55 \rightarrow 35 \rightarrow 23 \rightarrow 11 \rightarrow 3$ (1)

(d) $18 \rightarrow 17 \rightarrow 15 \rightarrow 11 \rightarrow 3$ (1)

(ii)   Answers vary; examples:

       18 and 81 follow the same route.

       The order of the digits makes no difference to the result.   (1)

(iii) (a)   29 → 29   (1)

      (b)   59 → 59   (1)

      (c)   95 → 59   (1)

(iv) These numbers have only one stage and do not reach a single-digit number.   (1)

(v)   34, 39, 43 and 45   (4)

(vi) 79   (2)

19 Tom's number is 13   (6)

20 (i)   Gaps filled in with missing palindromic prime numbers

       11   **101**   131   **151**   181   **191**   313   **353**   373   **383**   (5)

   (ii) (a)   All other two-digit palindromic numbers are multiples of 11   (1)

       (b)   They would all be even (end in 2)   (1)

       (c)   They would be even or multiples of 5   (2)

       (d)   707 divides by 7   (1)

       (e)   717 divides by 3   (1)

   (iii) 1009 is the smallest prime number greater than 1000
        1001 is 7 × 11 × 13, 1003 is 17 × 59, 1007 is 19 × 53   (2)

21 I II III V X XIX XX XXX L C CXC

    CC CCC D M MCM MM (MMM)   (3)

22 XIV (The numbers are III (3) and XVII (17))   (4)

23 (i)   LXVI × X = DCLX

       LXVI × I = LXVI

       DCLX + LXVI = DCLLXXVI = DCCXXVI   (4)

   (ii) XXX = VVVVVV

       VVVVVV = VVVVVIIIII

At this stage it is clear that VI will go into VVVVVIIIII five times,

so the answer is V   (4)

24 **(i)** Regular hexagon constructed and labelled (3)

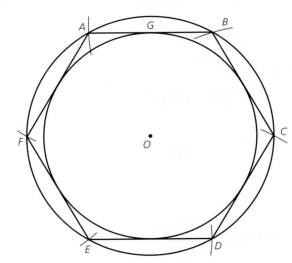

(ii) O and G labelled (1)

(iii) Circumscribed circle drawn (probably as part of construction) (2)
Inscribed circle drawn

(iv) 1.14 ($\frac{8}{7}$ or $1\frac{1}{7}$) (2)

→ 3.2 Real-life mathematics

1	**(a)**	£21.89	(2)			
	(b)	**(i)** £29.46	(2)	**(ii)**	£20.54	(2)
	(c)	£11.50	(2)			
2	**(i)**	**(a)** 56 m	(1)	**(b)**	192 m^2	(1)
	(ii)	**(a)** 10.5 m	(1)	**(b)**	183.75 m^2	(3)
3	**(a)**	$\frac{1}{3}$	(2)	**(b)**	$\frac{5}{12}$	(2)
	(c)	**(i)** 7	(1)	**(ii)**	6	(1)
4	**(i)**	List completed: 225 pence, 49 pence, 3 kg	(3)			
	(ii)	12 kg	(1)			
	(iii)	£6.40	(2)			
	(iv)	53 pence per kilogram	(2)			
5	**(i)**	3240 g	(2)			
	(ii)	**(a)** 1600 ml	(2)	**(c)**	1280 g (1.28 kg)	(2)
		(b) 8 eggs	(2)	**(d)**	1.6 kg (1600 g)	(2)
6	**(i)**	£392	(2)			
	(ii)	**(a)** £95	(1)	**(b)**	19%	(2)

7 (i) (a) $x + 7$ (1) (b) $2x + 5$ (1)

(ii) $2x + 5 = x + 10$ (2)

(iii) $x = 5$ (2)

(iv) 12 tokens (Anne has 12; Belinda has 15) (2)

8 (a) (i)   50 m/s (3) (ii) 110 miles/hour (2)

(b) 12:40 (4)

9 (a) 45 cm (2) (b) £15 (4)

10 (i) 50 copies (2)

(ii) (a) 3.2 cm (2)

(b) 37 copies ($37\frac{1}{2}$ so there is not room for 38 copies!) (3)

11 (i) (a) Range 7 centimetres (1)

(b) Range 13 square centimetres (1)

(c) Median 40 cm (1)

(d) Median 112 cm² (1)

(ii) Points plotted (3)

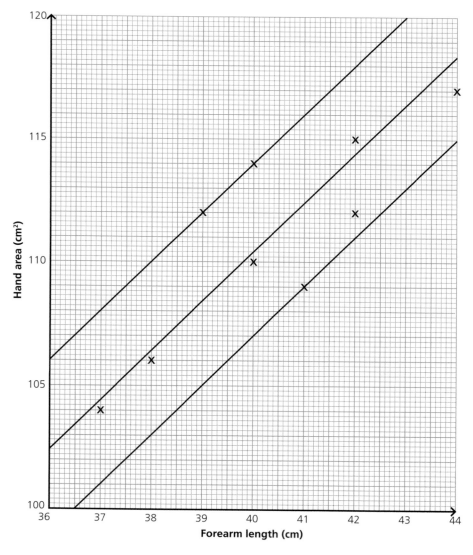

(iii)	Positive (and fairly high) correlation			(2)			

(iii) Positive (and fairly high) correlation (2)

(iv) (a) Line of best fit drawn (1) (b) Parallel lines drawn (2)

(v) (a) About 99 cm^2 (1) (b) About 106 cm^2 (1)

(vi) Shanna's hand area approximately 100 cm^2 (3)

12 (i) 250 miles (2) (iii) 240 miles (2)

(ii) 84 litres (2) (iv) 28 litres (2)

13 (i) $\frac{5}{6}$ (2)

(ii) $\frac{1}{6}$ (1)

(iii) 54 (number must be a multiple of 6) (2)

(iv) Charles took 9 more stamps than Hannah. (2)

14 (i) (a) $\frac{1}{10}$ (1) (b) $\frac{3}{10}$ (1)

(ii) $\frac{3}{5}$ (1)

(iii) $\frac{9}{20}$ (2)

(iv) 80 (2)

(v)

Grade	A	B	C	D	E
Number of candidates	8	24	36	5	7

(3)

15 (i) 252 (2) (iv) $\frac{4}{9}$ (2)

(ii) 450 (1) (v) 56% (2)

(iii) 5 : 4 (2)

16 (i) 8 km (1) (iv) 54 litres (2)

(ii) 15 litres (1) (v) £67.50 (3)

(iii) 144 km (1)

17 (i) 90 cm (88 cm + 2 cm) (3) (iii) 4312 cm^3 (2)

(ii) 616 cm^2 (3) (iv) 5488 cm^3 (2)

18 (a) (i) 140 metres (1) (ii) 714 complete revolutions (1)

(b) (i) 22.5 km (22 500 metres) (2) (ii) 9.5 tonnes (9500 kg) (2)

19 (i) 16 m^2 (1) (iii) 9 m^2 (3)

(ii) 4.8 m^3 (2)

20 (i) 154 cm^2 (3)

(ii) (a) 784 cm^2 (1) (c) 476 cm^2 (2)

(b) 308 cm^2 (2)

(iii) 39% (2)

21	(i)	5 cm		(1)
	(ii)	(a)	$20x - 200$ or $20(x - 10)$ cm²	(2)
		(b)	$(30x - 100)$ cm²	(4)
	(iii)	(a)	$x = 48$	(2)
		(b)	1340 cm² (0.134 m²)	(2)

22 (i) (a) 500 m (2)   (b) $\frac{1}{2}$ km (0.5 km) (1)

    (ii) $2\frac{1}{4}$ km (2.25 km) (2)   (iii) 27 minutes (3)

23 (i) 1500 litres (1.5 m³) (3)

    (ii) 75 days (3)

    (iii) (a) 100 litres (1)   (b) 1.4 m (3)

24 (i) 81 000 (2)

    (ii) 24 300 (2)

    (iii) 32 400 (England had 56 700 supporters) (2)

25 (i) 1.6 g (2)

    (ii) (a) 400 cm² (1)   (b) 360 cm² (1)

    (iii) (a) 6.4 g (2)   (b) 5.76 g (2)

26 (i) 22 litres (2)   (iii) 26 litres (2)

    (ii) 585 miles (2)

27 (i) 9 screws (1)   (iv) 57 screws (2)

    (ii) 17 screws (2)   (v) 121 screws (1)

    (iii) 38 screws (3)

28 (i) 18% (2)   (iii) £95.20 (2)

    (ii) £120.21 (2)   (iv) 33 266.91 kWh (2)

                                           (£1347.31 spent on gas)

29 Invoice completed (bold entries) (6)

	Quantity	Unit price (£)	Total price (£)
Account payments			
Cheques	4	0.70	2.80
Direct Debits	17	0.40	**6.80**
Free Debits	1	0.00	0.00
Subtotal			9.60
Account receipts			
Automated Credits	**15**	0.15	2.25
Credits paid in	2	**0.70**	1.40
Subtotal			3.65
Other services			
Cash paid in	560.00	0.47 per £100	**2.63**
Subtotal			**2.63**
Service total			**15.88**

30 **(i)** £370 (1)

(ii) £640 (2)

(iii) £11890 (3)
(£11520 + £370)

Algebra

→ 4.1 Equations and formulae

1 (a) $3a$ (1)
  (b) a (1)
  (c) $4a$ (1)
  (d) $2a^2$ (1)
  (e) a (1)

2 (a) $2a$ (1)
  (b) 0 (2)
  (c) $10c^3$ (2)
  (d) $2d$ (2)

3 (a) $6d$ (1)
  (b) $5d$ (1)
  (c) $12d^2$ (2)
  (d) $4d$ (1)

4 (a) $4m - 4$ (2)
  (b) $4(m - 1)$ (2)

5 (a) (i) $11y$ (1)
      (ii) $21y^3$ (2)
      (iii) $2y^2$ (1)
  (b) $6p - q$ (3)
  (c) $6(2a + 3b)$ (2)

6 (a) (i) $7p$ (1)
      (ii) $12p^2$ (2)
      (iii) p (2)
  (b) $3(3p - 2)$ (2)

7 (a) $13a$ (1)
  (b) ^-3a (2)
  (c) $40a^2$ (2)
  (d) $4a$ (2)
  (e) $25a^2$ (2)

8 (a) $2a + 23c$ (3)
  (b) $5p(p - 2q)$ (2)

9 (a) $3a + 7b$ (1)
  (b) $6a^2b$ (1)
  (c) ^-c (2)
  (d) $2d$ (2)
  (e) $6e^5$ (2)
  (f) $6e^2$ (2)

10 (a) $5x^2 - x^3$ (2)
   (b) $30x^2$ (2)
   (c) 2 (2)

11 (a) (i) $5x^3$ (1)
       (ii) $6x^6$ (2)
       (iii) $\dfrac{2x^2}{y^3}$ (2)
   (b) (i) $2s(s + 1)$ (2)
       (ii) $2r(2r - 3s)$ (2)

12 (a) $3x - y$ (3)

(b) (i) $6a^2$ (2)   (ii) b (2)

(c) $5a^2(a - 1)$ (2)

13 (a) $6a + 13$ (3)

(b) (i) $2(2a + 7)$ (1)   (ii) $\pi r(6 + r)$ (3)

14 (a) $5p + 2q$ (2)

(b) (i) $4p^2q^3$ (2)   (ii) $\dfrac{3p^2}{2q}$ (3)

15 (a) $\dfrac{3x - 12}{4x}$ (2)   (b) $2xy$ (2)

16 (i) 13 (2)   (iii) $^-7$ (2)

(ii) 10 (2)

17 (i) 13 (2)   (iii) $^-6$ (2)

(ii) 4 (2)

18 (i) 16 (2)   (iii) $^-96$ (3)

(ii) 15 (2)

19 (i) $^-1$ (2)   (iii) $^-12$ (2)

(ii) $^-10$ (2)

20 (i) 3 (2)   (iii) $^-3$ (2)

(ii) 0 (2)   (iv) $^-12$ (3)

21 (i) 0 (1)   (iii) $^-18$ (2)

(ii) 8 (2)

22 (a) (i) 0.64 (2)   (ii) 1.06 (3)

(b) 4.2 unit^2 (3)

23 (a) (i) $^-0.2$ (2)   (ii) $^-2.24$ (2)

(b) 46.2 cm^3 (3)

24 (i) (a) $4t$ (1)   (b) $4t + 4$ (1)

(ii) $4t + 4 = 44$ (2)

(iii) $t = 10$ (2)

(iv) 30 years (2)

25 (i) $n - 4$ (1)

(ii) (a) $5n$ (1)   (b) $7n - 4$ (2)

(iii) $n = 2$ (2)

26 (i) $\dfrac{x}{2}$ (1)   (iii) $x + \dfrac{x}{2} + \left(\dfrac{x}{2} + 30\right)$ which simplifies to $2x + 30$ (2)

(ii) $\dfrac{x}{2} + 30$ (1)   (iv) $2x + 30 = 180 \rightarrow x = 75$ (2)

(v) (a) Angle Q is 37.5° (1)   (b) Angle R is 67.5° (1)

27 (i) cn (pence) (1)

   (ii) (a) $c - 5 = d$ (2)   (b) $c = 14$ (2)

   (iii) $n = 39$ (pence) (2)

   (iv) £5.46 (1)

28 (i) (a) $r + 3$ (1)   (b) $4r$ (1)

   (ii) (a) $6r + 3$ (2)   (b) $2r + 1$ (2)

   (iii) $2r + 1 = 11 \rightarrow r = 5$ (3)

   (iv) 5, 8, 20 (1)

29 (i) $2 : 3$ (2)

   (ii) (a) $2x$ (1)   (b) $3x$ (1)

   (iii) $\frac{2}{3}$ (2)

   (iv) (a) 42 (2)   (b) 14 (2)

30 (a) $w = 9$ (1)   (c) $y = 8$ (2)

   (b) $x = 4$ (1)   (d) $z = 3$ (2)

31 (a) $a = 5$ (1)   (c) $c = 3$ (2)

   (b) $b = 48$ (2)   (d) $d = 6$ (3)

32 (a) $w = 15$ (1)   (c) $y = 8$ (2)

   (b) $x = 7$ (2)   (d) $z = {}^{-}2$ (3)

33 (a) $v = 3$ (1)   (c) $x = 10$ (2)

   (b) $w = 28$ (2)   (d) $y = {}^{-}18$ (3)

34 (a) $x = -6$ (2)   (c) $z = 5$ (3)

   (b) $y = 3$ (2)

35 (a) $x = 10$ (1)   (c) $z = 7$ (2)

   (b) $y = 4$ (2)

36 $z = 14$ (4)

37 (a) $p = -1$ (1)   (c) $r = 20$ (2)

   (b) $q = 3\frac{1}{2}$ (2)   (d) $s = 3$ (3)

38 (a) $x = 11$ (2)   (c) $z = {}^{-}\frac{1}{4}$ (2)

   (b) $y = 10$ (2)

39 (a) $a = 5$ (2)   (c) $c = 11$ (3)

   (b) $b = 10\frac{1}{2}$ (2)

40 (a) (i) $x = 18$ (2)   (iii) $z = 17$ (3)

      (ii) $y = {}^{-}3$ (3)

   (b) (i) $a > 2$ (2)   (ii) $b < 10\frac{2}{3}$ (3)

41 (a) (i) $x \leq 8$ (2) (ii) 1, 2, 3, 4, 5, 6, 7, 8 (2)

    (b) (i) $x > 4$ (2) (ii) 5, 6, 7, 8 (2)

42 (i) $x > -3$ (2) (ii) $-2, -1$ (2)

43 (a) $x = 2$ (2)

    (b) (i) $p < 6\frac{2}{3}$ (2) (ii) 1, 2, 3, 4, 5, 6 (1)

44 (i) (a) $x < 3$ (2) (b) $x \geq -2$ (3)

    (ii) $-2, -1, 0, 1, 2$ (1)

45 (a) (i) $2a^2$ (2) (ii) 1 (2)

    (b) $4a(2a + 3)$ (2)

    (c) $9a - 26b$ (2)

    (d) (i) $a < 3\frac{1}{5}$ (2) (ii) 1, 2, 3 (1)

46 (a) (i) $x = 28$ (2) (ii) $w = 5\frac{1}{3}$ (2)

    (b) $4x^2 - 5x + 18$ (4)

    (c) (i) $x > 4\frac{1}{2}$ (3) (iii) Number line drawn (2)

         (ii) $x < 12$ (3)

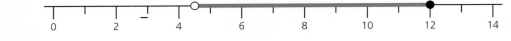

47 $x = 5.91$ (4)

48 $x = 1.53$ (5)

49 $x = 7$ or $x = 3$ (5)

50 (i) (a) $w + 5.3$ (1) (b) $w(w + 5.3)$ (2)

    (ii) (a) 9.78 cm (4) (b) 28.52 cm (3)

51 (i) (a) $\frac{48}{b}$ (2) (b) $\frac{48}{b} - b$ (3)

    (ii) (a) 2.4 (2) (c) 17.6 (1)

         (b) 20 (1)

52 (i) $x + 4$ (1)

    (ii) $x(x + 4) \rightarrow x^2 + 4x$ (2)

    (iii) $x^2 + 4x = 50 \rightarrow x = 5.35$ (5)

53 (a) $x = 2.5$ cm (3)

    (b) (i) 2 faces area $x(x - 2) \rightarrow 2x^2 - 4x$

              2 faces area $4(x - 2) \rightarrow 8x - 16$

              2 faces area $4x \rightarrow 8x$

              Total surface area $2x^2 + 12x - 16$ (4)

         (ii) $2x^2 + 12x - 16 = 94 \rightarrow 2x^2 + 12x - 110 = 0$ (1)

         (iii) $x = 5$ (The second solution to this equation, -11, is not
                appropriate in this case!) (3)

54 (i) (a) $x < 8\frac{1}{3}$ (2) (b) $x \geq {}^-6$ (2)

(ii) $^-6, {}^-5, {}^-4, {}^-3, {}^-2, {}^-1, 0, 1, 2, 3, 4, 5, 6, 7, 8$ (3)

55 (i) $x(5x + 2)$ (2)

(ii) $x = {}^-2$ and $x = 1.6$ (8)

56 (a) $2x(2x + 1)$ (2)

(b) (i) $2x(x + 3\frac{1}{2}) = {}^-4$ (2)

(ii) $^-2.78$ (6)

→ 4.2   Sequences and functions

1 (a) 29, 23 (2) (c) 16, 8 (2)

(b) 21, 25 (2)

2 (a) (i) 24 (1) (ii) 32 (1)

(b) (i) 19 (1) (ii) 25 (1)

(c) (i) 21 (2) (ii) 144 (2)

3 (a) 30, 37 (2) (c) $3\frac{1}{2}, 1\frac{1}{4}$ (4)

(b) 81, 243 (2)

4 (a) 126, 626, 3126 (3) (b) (4), 6, 12, 30, 84 (4)

5 (a) $\frac{6}{7}, \frac{5}{6}$ (2) (c) 111, 37 (2)

(b) 35, 17 (2)

6 (a) (i) 27, 35 (2) (iii) 23, 37 (2)

(ii) 100, 144 (2)

(b) (i) 16 (1) (iii) $3n - 2$ (2)

(ii) 28 (1) (iv) 298 (2)

7 (i) 17, 20 (1) (iv) 41 (2)

(ii) $3n + 2$ (2) (v) 333rd term = 1001 (2)

(iii) 62 (1)

8 (i) (a) $^-4$ (1) (b) 9995 (1)

(ii) $n = 23$ (2)

9 (i) (a) $\frac{1}{7}$ (1) (b) $\frac{199}{601}$ (1)

(ii) t_n approaches $\frac{1}{3}$ (2)

10 (i) $\frac{10^2}{4} \rightarrow \frac{100}{4} \rightarrow 25$ (2)

(ii)

T_n	Sequence	1st difference sequence	nth term of 1st difference	2nd difference constant	
$\frac{1}{4}n$	$\frac{1}{4}, 1, 2\frac{1}{4}, 4, \ldots$	$\frac{3}{4}, 1\frac{1}{4}, 1\frac{3}{4}, \ldots$	$\frac{1}{2}\left(n+\frac{1}{2}\right)$	$\frac{1}{2}$	
$\frac{1}{2}n$	$\frac{1}{2}, 2, 4\frac{1}{2}, 8, \ldots$	$1\frac{1}{2}, 2\frac{1}{2}, 3\frac{1}{2}, \ldots$	$n + \frac{1}{2}$	1	
n^2	1, 4, 9, 16, …	3, 5, 7, …	$2n + 1$	2	(4)
$2n^2$	2, 8, 18, 32, …	6, 10, 16, …	$4n + 2$	4	(4)

11 **(a)** $x = 3$ drawn and labelled on grid   (1)

(b) $y = 5$ drawn and labelled   (1)

(c) $x = {}^-4$ drawn and labelled   (1)

(d) $y = x$ drawn and labelled   (2)

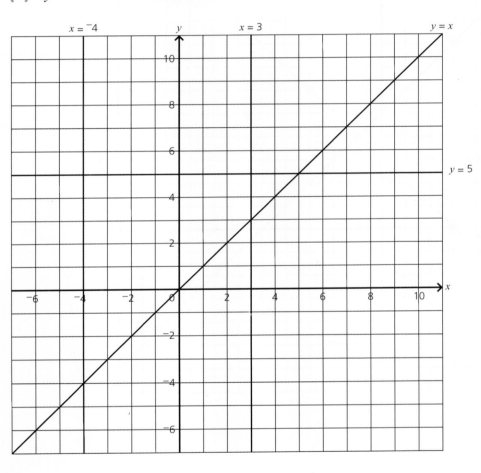

12　(i)　(a)　　　　　　　　　　　　　　　　　　　　　　　　　　　　　　　(2)

x	-3	0	3
y	0	3	6

(b)　Graph of $y = x + 3$ drawn on grid　　　　　　　　　　　　　(2)

(ii)　(a)　　　　　　　　　　　　　　　　　　　　　　　　　　　　　　　(2)

x	-3	0	3
y	8	5	2

(b)　Graph of $y = 5 - x$ drawn on grid　　　　　　　　　　　　　(1)

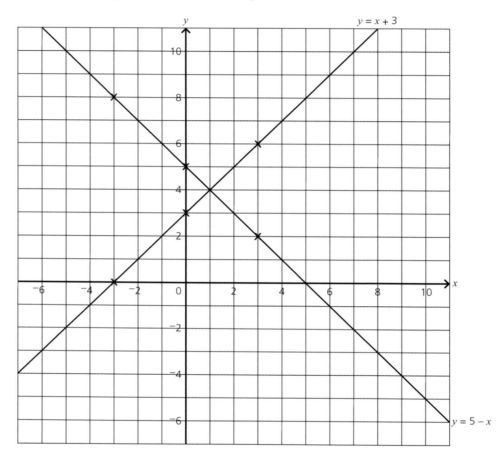

(iii)　(1, 4)　　　　　　　　　　　　　　　　　　　　　　　　　　　　　(2)

13 **(i)** **(a)** (2)

x	-2	1	4
y	-1	2	5

(b) (2)

x	-2	1	4
y	9	6	3

(ii) **(a)** Graph of $y = x + 1$ drawn (1)

(b) Graph of $y = 7 - x$ drawn (2)

(iii) Line $y = 1$ drawn (1)

(iv) 4 points circled (2)

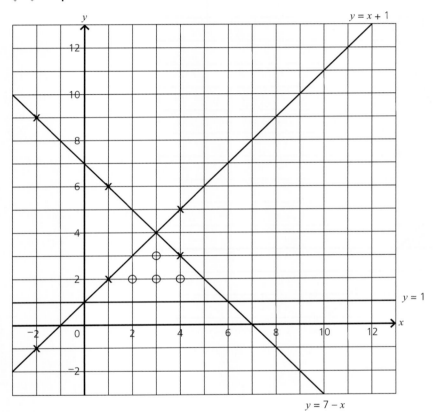

14 **(i)** Answers vary; examples (0, 3), (2, 1) (2)

(ii) $y = {}^-1$ (1)

(iii) **(a)** (2)

x	$^-1$	0	1	2	x
y	1	3	5	7	**2x + 3**

(b) $y = 2x + 3$ (1)

(c) Line C ($y = 2x + 3$) drawn (2)

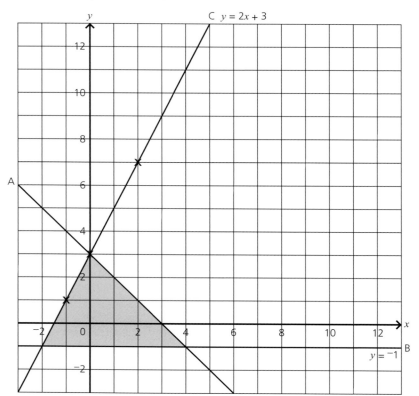

(iv) 12 cm² (3)

15 **(i)** 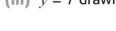 (2)

x	-3	-2	-1	0	1	2	3
y	9	4	1	0	1	4	9

(ii) Graph of $y = x^2$ drawn (2)

(iii) $y = 7$ drawn (1)

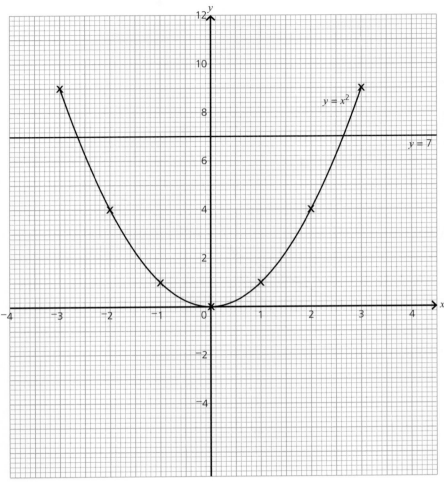

(iv) 2.65 (1)

16 **(i)** (2)

x	⁻3	⁻2	⁻1	0	1	2	3
y	7	2	⁻1	⁻2	⁻1	2	7

(ii) Graph of $y = x^2 - 2$ drawn (2)

(iii) $y = x$ drawn (2)

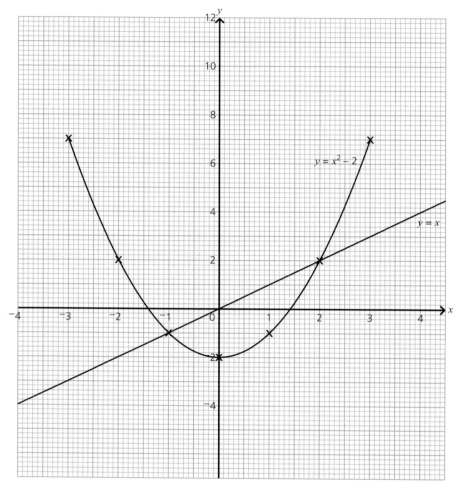

(iv) (⁻1, ⁻1), (2, 2) (2)

17 (i) (3)

x	$^-3$	$^-2$	$^-1$	0	1	2	3	4
$\frac{1}{2}x^2$	4.5	2	0.5	0	0.5	2	4.5	8
y	1.5	$^-1$	$^-2.5$	$^-3$	$^-2.5$	$^-1$	1.5	5

(ii) Graph of $y = \frac{1}{2}x^2 - 3$ drawn (2)

(iii) Graph of $y = x - 1$ drawn (3)

(iv) Points circled (1)

(v) $(1, {}^-2)$ (1)

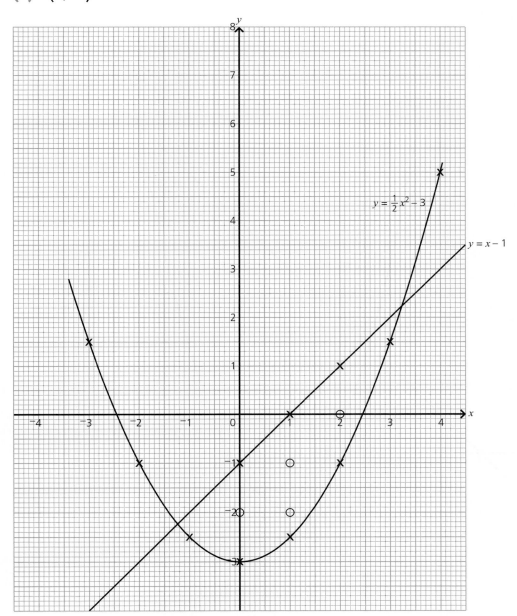

18 (i)

x	-2	-1	$\frac{-1}{2}$	0	$\frac{1}{2}$	1	$1\frac{1}{2}$	2	3	4
y	8	3	$1\frac{1}{4}$	0	$\frac{-3}{4}$	-1	$\frac{-3}{4}$	0	3	8

(3)

(ii) Graph of $y = x^2 - 2x$ drawn (2)

(iii)

x	-3	0	3
y	0	3	6

(2)

(iv) Graph of $y = x + 3$ drawn (1)

(v) (3.75, 6.75) (2)

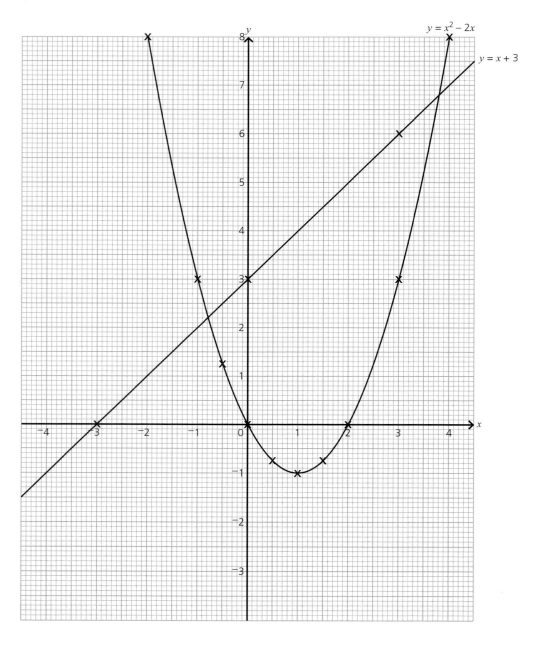

19 **(i)** **(a)** (2)

x	-2	-1	0	1	2
y	4	1	0	1	4

(b) (2)

x	-2	-1	0	1	2
y	-1	2	3	2	-1

(ii) Two graphs drawn (4)

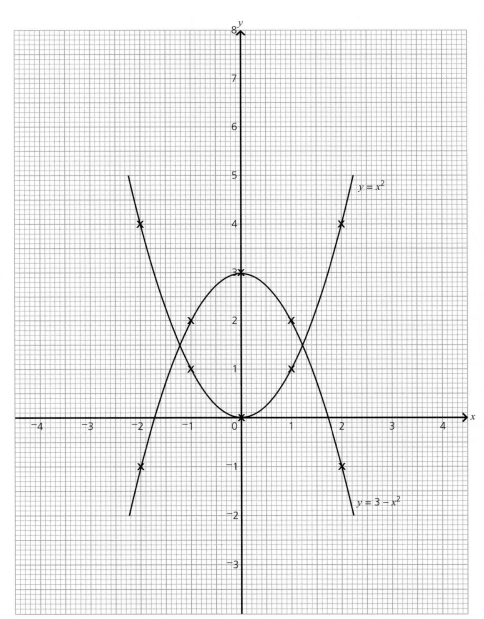

(iii) (-1.2, 1.5) (1.2, 1.5) (4)

20 **(i)** (3)

Input (x)	Output (y)
−1	0
2	6
4	10

(ii) Graph of function drawn and labelled (3)

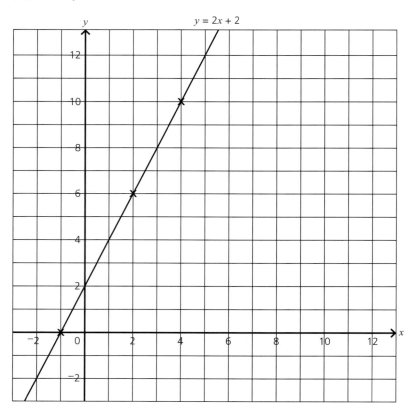

21 **(i)** Labels written on machine (2)

(ii) 13 (2)

22 **(i)** (4)

x	−3	−2	−1	0	1	2	3
x²	9	4	1	0	1	4	9
y	6	2	0	0	2	6	12

(ii) **(a)** y has its lowest value when x is $-\frac{1}{2}$ (1)

(b) The lowest value of y is $\frac{-1}{4}$ (1)

(iii) Graph drawn (3)

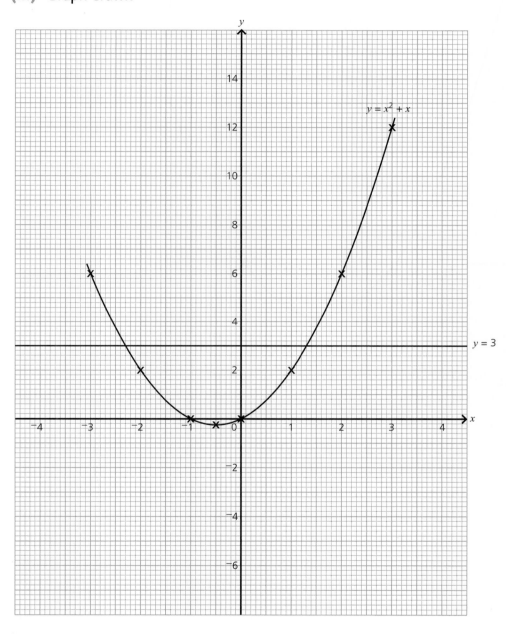

(iv) −2.3 and 1.3 (2)

23 **(i)** $x = \dfrac{1}{2}$ (1)

(ii) $\left(\dfrac{1}{2}, \; ^{-}2\dfrac{1}{4} \right)$ (2)

(iii) **(a)** Point plotted (1)

(b) Graph drawn (2)

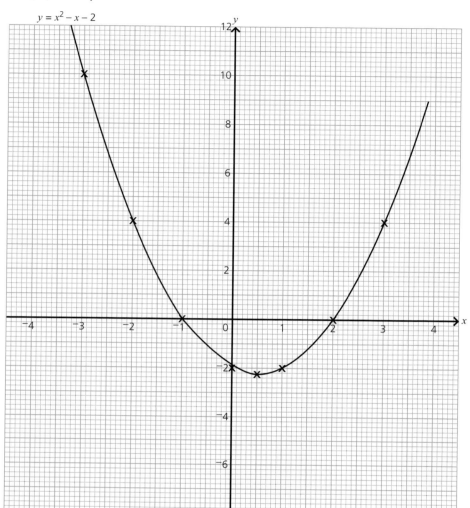

24 (i) (5)

x	$^-3$	$^-2$	$^-1$	0	$\frac{1}{2}$	1	2	3	4
x^2	9	4	1	0	$\frac{1}{4}$	1	4	9	16
$\frac{1}{2}x^2$	$4\frac{1}{2}$	2	$\frac{1}{2}$	0	$\frac{1}{8}$	$\frac{1}{2}$	2	$4\frac{1}{2}$	8
$\frac{1}{2}x$	$^-1\frac{1}{2}$	$^-1$	$^-\frac{1}{2}$	0	$\frac{1}{4}$	$\frac{1}{2}$	1	$1\frac{1}{2}$	2
y	6	3	1	0	$\frac{^-1}{8}$	0	1	3	6

(ii) Graph drawn (3)

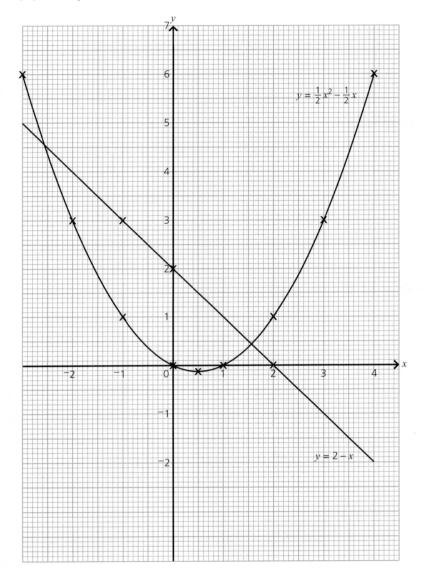

$y = \frac{1}{2}x^2 - \frac{1}{2}x$

$y = 2 - x$

(iii) (a) (2)

x	$^-1$	0	2
y	3	2	0

(b) $y = 2 - x$ drawn (1)

(iv) approximately ($^-2.5$, 4.5) and (1.5, 0.5) since these reasonably satisfy both equations (2)

37

25 (i) Tables completed

(a) Machine P: $y = x^2 - 1$ (2)

Input (x)	Output (y)
2	3
⁻3	8

(b) Machine Q: $y = (x - 1)^2$ (2)

Input (x)	Output (y)
2	1
⁻3	16

(c) Machine R: $y = x^2 - 2x + 1$ (3)

Input (x)	Output (y)
2	1
⁻3	16

(ii) $(x - 1)^2$ is equivalent to $x^2 - 2x + 1$ (2)

26 (i) (a) $m + n$ (1)   **(b)** $n - m$ (1)

(ii) $m + n = 25$ (2)

(iii) $n = 16$ (3)

27 $x = 12, y = 4$ (4)

28 $a = 7, b = 2$ (4)

29 (i) $2(x + y) = 22$ or $2x + 2y = 22$ and $x - y = 1$ (3)

(ii) $x = 6, y = 5$ (3)

30 $x = 2, y = ⁻3$ (5)

31 (i) $x + y = 43$ and $x - y = 30$ (4)

(ii) $x = 36.5, y = 6.5$ (3)

(iii) 237.25   (2)

32 (i) (a) 41   (2)   **(b)** 54   (2)

(ii) The 11th term 149   (3)

(iii) The first term 9   (2)

33 (i) (a) $100x + 50y = 850$ (2)   **(b)** $50x + 100y = 950$ (2)

(ii) (a) $x = 5$ (2)   **(b)** $y = 7$ (2)

34 (a) $x = \frac{1}{4}, \; y = 2$ (5)

(b) (i) 17   (3)   **(ii)** 731   (2)

Geometry and measures

→ 5.1 Measures

1	(a)	350 cm	(1)		(c)	4050 ml	(1)
	(b)	73.6 cm	(1)		(d)	0.69 kg	(1)
2	(a)	12.4 degrees	(2)		(c)	1.24	(1)
	(b)	2.5 inches	(1)				
3	(i)	400 g	(2)		(iii)	8000 cm³	(2)
	(ii)	70 cm	(2)				

4   (i)   Triangle *ABC* constructed   (4)

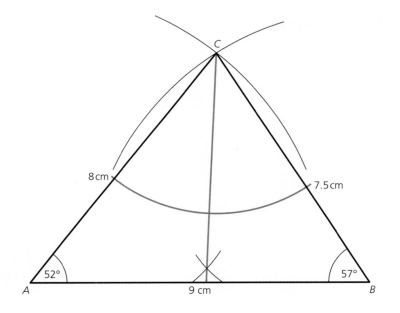

(ii)	(a)	57°	(1)	(b)	52°	(1)
(iii)	Bisector of angle *ACB* constructed					(2)

5 **(i)** Triangle *ABC* constructed (3)

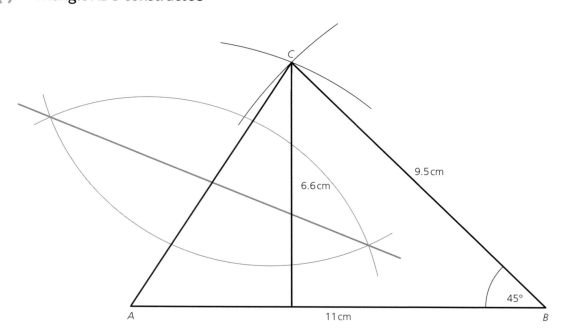

(ii) 6.6 cm (1)

(iii) Perpendicular bisector of *AC* constructed (2)

6 **(i)** 30°, 60°, 90° (2)

(ii) (2)

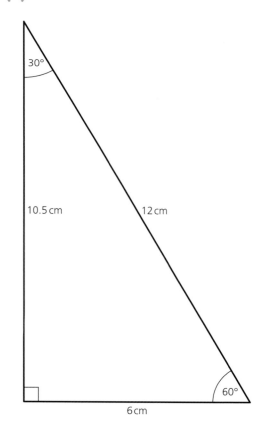

(iii) 31.5 cm² (2)

7 **(i)** Triangle *ABC* constructed (2)

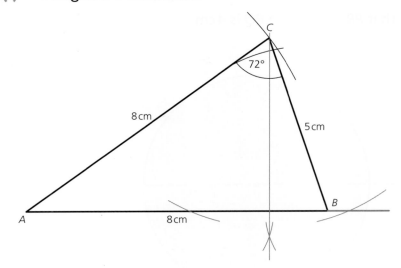

(ii) 72° (1)

(iii) Perpendicular to *AB* passing through *C* constructed (2)

8 **(i)** Regular hexagon *ABCDEF* constructed (3)

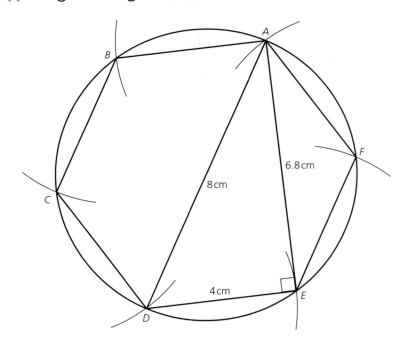

(ii) 8 cm (1)

(iii) About 40–41 cm² (3)

9 (i)   Line *PQ*, 12 cm long, drawn   (2)

   (ii)   Point *R* marked, such that *PR* is 8 cm and *RQ* is 4 cm   (2)

   (iii) Area represented   (3)

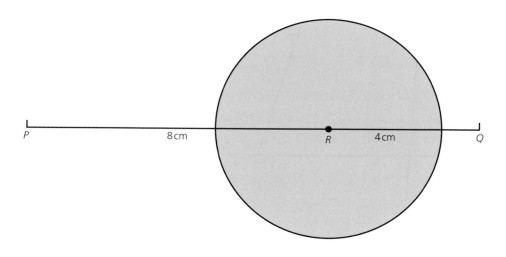

10 (i)   Square drawn   (3)

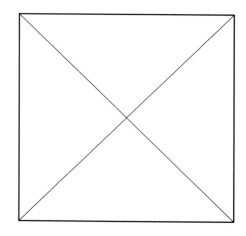

    (ii)   5.7 cm   (1)

    (iii) (a) 22.8 cm   (2)

           (b) 32.5 cm²   (2)

11 (a)   (i)   12 cm²   (2)

          (ii) 18 cm   (2)

    (b)   (i)   14 cm²   (2)

          (ii) 22 cm   (1)

12 **(i)** Cuboid drawn (3)

(ii) 90 cm³	(2)	**(iii)** 126 cm²	(4)
13 (i) 36 cm³	(2)	**(ii)** 70 cm²	(4)
14 (i) 477 cm³	(3)		
(ii) (a) 250 cm³	(2)	**(b)** 227 cm³	(1)
15 (i) 500 m	(2)		
(ii) 38 cm	(2)		
(iii) 3.25 km	(2)		
(iv) (a) 50 000 m²	(3)	**(b)** 5 ha	(1)
16 (i) 36 mm	(2)	**(iii)** 150 mm³	(2)
(ii) 100 mm²	(3)		
17 (i) (a) 88 cm	(2)	**(b)** 616 cm²	(3)
(ii) (a) 462 cm²	(2)	**(b)** 300 g	(3)
18 (a) 1.54 m²	(2)	**(c)** 1540 cm³	(2)
(b) 390 cm³	(2)		
19 (i) 14 m	(1)	**(iv)** 56 m²	(3)
(ii) 280 m²	(1)	**(v)** 68 m²	(3)
(iii) 154 m²	(2)	**(vi)** 124 m²	(1)
20 (i) (a) 3.5 cm	(2)	**(b)** 38.5 cm²	(2)
(ii) 423.5 cm³	(2)		
(iii) 2.75 cm	(3)		

| 21 | (i) | (a) | 18 cm² | (2) | (b) | 30 cm² | (2) |

21 (i) (a) 18 cm²   (2)   (b) 30 cm²   (2)
    (ii) 4.8 cm   (1)
    (iii) (a) 30.1 cm   (3)   (b) 10.0 cm   (2)
    (iv) 300 sheep   (2)
22 (i) 8 m/s   (2)   (ii) 28.8 km/h   (3)
23 (a) A solid shape which has:

- three or more parallel edges of equal length
- constant cross-section   (3)

    (b) 15.7 m³   (4)

→ 5.2 Shape

1 (i)   (2)

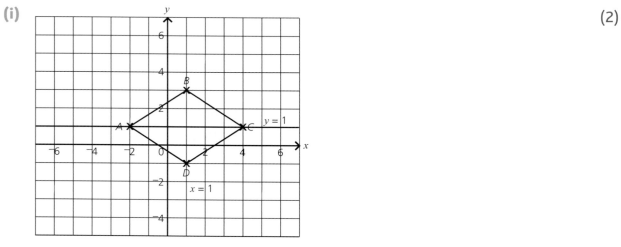

    (ii) (a) Points joined to form *ABCD*   (1)
          (b) Rhombus   (1)
    (iii) (a) Two lines of symmetry drawn   (1)
          (b) $x = 1$ and $y = 1$ (1)
    (iv) Order 2   (1)
    (v)   12 cm²   (2)
2 (a) (i) Square with lines of symmetry drawn   (1)

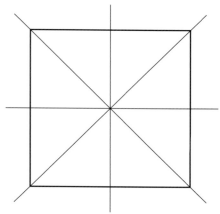

        (ii)   4 lines of symmetry drawn   (2)
        (iii) Order 4   (1)

(b) **(i)** Isosceles trapezium or kite sketched (2)

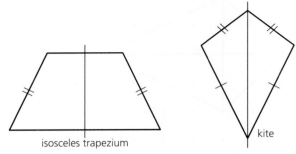

isosceles trapezium   kite

(ii) Isosceles trapezium or kite (1)

3 **(a)** **(i)** (4)

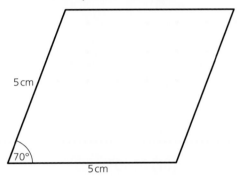

5 cm

70°

5 cm

(ii) Rhombus (1)

(b) **(i)** No lines of symmetry

Rotational symmetry order 2 (2)

(ii) Opposite sides parallel (1)

(iii) Opposite angles equal (1)

4 **(i)** 45° (2) **(iii)** 1080° (1)

(ii) 8 sides (2) **(iv)** Regular octagon (1)

5 **(a)** 144° (3)

(b) **(i)** Regular pentagon (2)

(ii) Order 5 (1)

6 **(i)** **(a)** 9 sides (1) **(c)** 1260° (1)

(b) 140° (1)

(ii) **(a)** 40° (2) **(b)** 30° (2)

7 **(i)** **(a)** 8 vertices (2) **(b)** 12 edges (2)

(ii) **(a)** 10 cm² (2) **(c)** 20 cm³ (2)

(b) 51.2 cm² (2)

8 Answers vary; examples: (2 marks each)

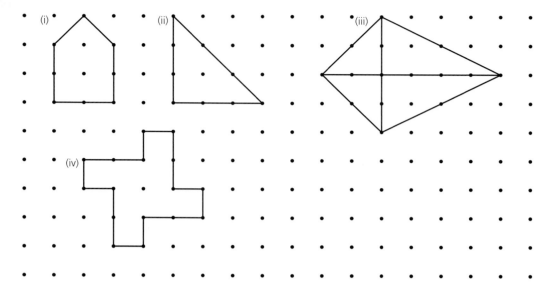

→ 5.3 Space

1 (i)   50°   (2)   (iii) 140°   (1)
   (ii) 40°   (2)

2 (a) (i)   48°   (1)   (ii) 132°   (2)
   (b) (i)   36°   (2)   (ii) 108°   (2)

3 (i)   125°   (1)   (iv) 70°   (1)
   (ii) 70°   (2)   (v)   140°   (2)
   (iii) 70°   (2)

4 (i)   60°   (1)   (iii) 30°   (2)
   (ii) 120°   (1)   (iv) 90°   (2)

5 (i) (a)   35°   (1)   (c)   110°   (2)
       (b)   25°   (1)   (d)   120°   (2)
   (ii) Trapezium   (1)

6 (i)   45°   (1)   (iii) 35°   (2)
   (ii) 145°   (2)   (iv) 235°   (2)

7 (i)   35°   (1)   (iv) 80°   (2)
   (ii) 70°   (1)   (v)   145°   (2)
   (iii) 110°   (2)

8 (i) (a)   1 cm to represent 2 km   (1)
       (b)   1 : 200 000   (2)
   (ii) Diagram copied   (2)
   (iii) Rulerford marked   (2)

46

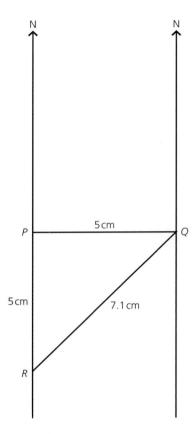

(iv) (a)   10 km   (1)

     (b)   14.2 km   (2)

9 (i)   C marked and north line drawn through it   (1)

   (ii)   L marked   (2)

   (iii) F marked   (2)

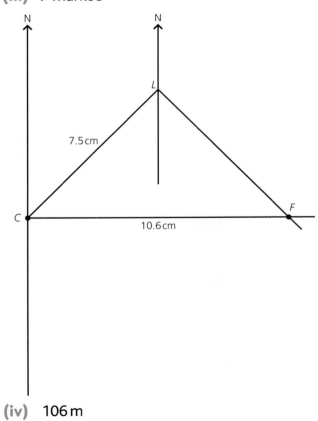

(iv) 106 m   (2)

10 **(i)** (4)

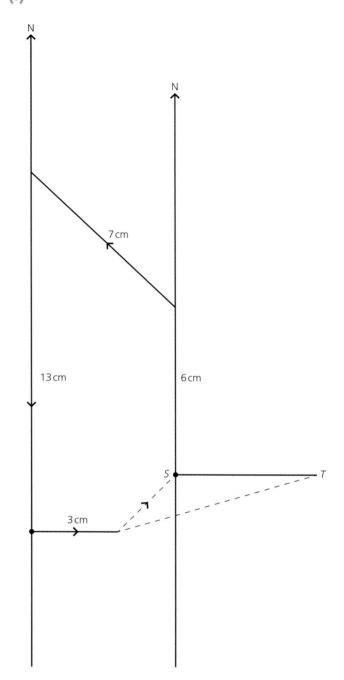

(ii) **(a)** 7 paces (2)

(b) Approximately NE (2)

11 **(i)** 030° (1) **(iii)** 210° (2)

(ii) 108° (2)

12 **(i)** 100° (2) **(ii)** 245° (3)

13 (i) Route of boat drawn (2)

(ii) Position of *W* marked (2)

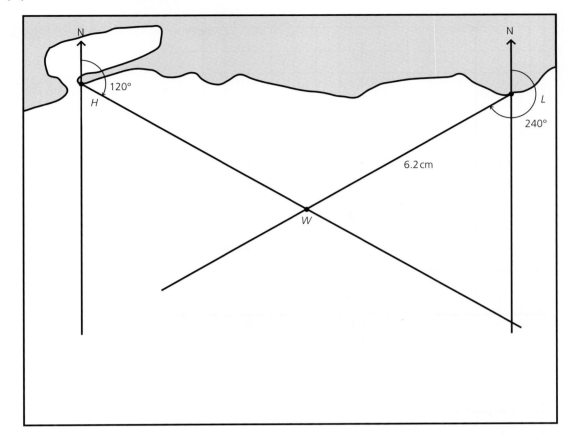

(iii) 310 m (3)

14 (i) (4)

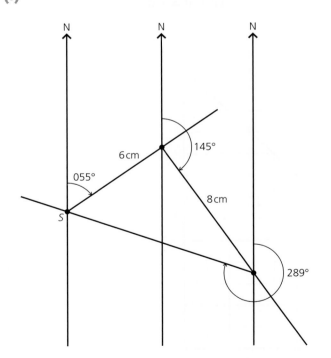

(ii) 90° (1) **(iv)** 289° (2)

(iii) 100 m (3)

15 **(i)** Triangle **A** drawn (2) **(iii)** Triangle **B** drawn (3)

   (ii) Line $y = 2$ drawn (1) **(iv)** (3, ⁻1), (6, 1), (8, ⁻2) (3)

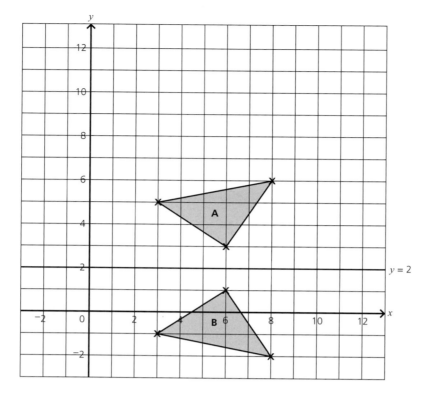

16 **(i)** Point *A* plotted (1)

   (ii) Point *B* plotted (1)

   (iii) Point *C* plotted (1)

   (iv) **(a)** Triangle *ABC* drawn (1)   **(b)** Line $y = x$ drawn (1)

   (v) Triangle *A'B'C'* drawn (4)

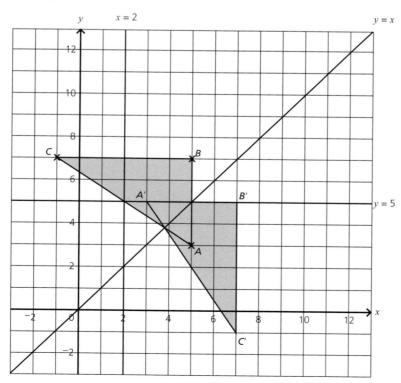

17 **(i)** Points plotted and triangle
     A drawn   (1)
   (ii) Line $y = 6$ drawn,   (1)
   (iii) Triangle **B** drawn   (2)

   (iv) Triangle **C** drawn   (2)
   (v) Triangle **D** drawn   (1)

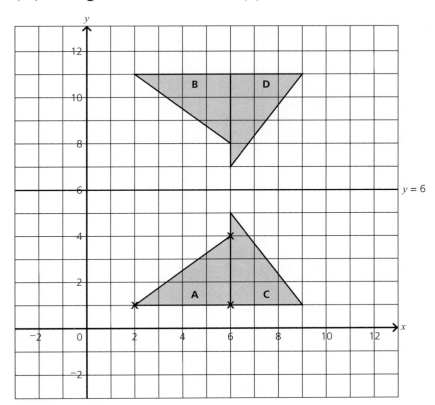

18 **(i)** Triangle **P** drawn   (2)
   (ii) Triangle **Q** drawn   (2)

   (iii) Triangle **R** drawn   (2)
   (iv) Line $y = x$ drawn   (2)

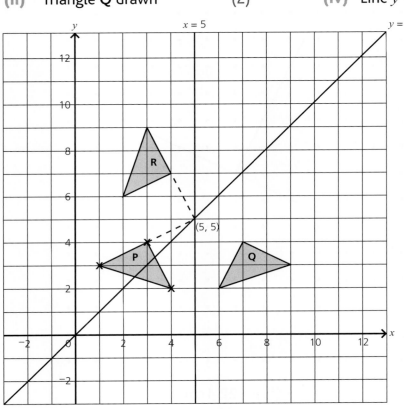

19 (4)

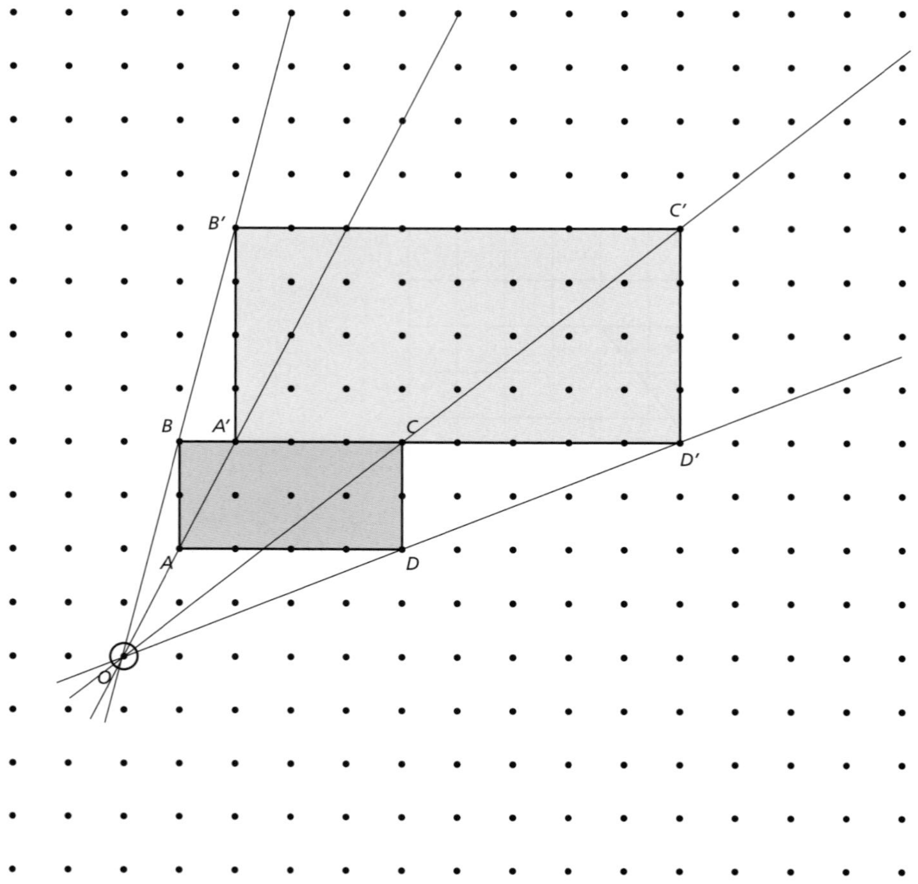

20 (i) (3)

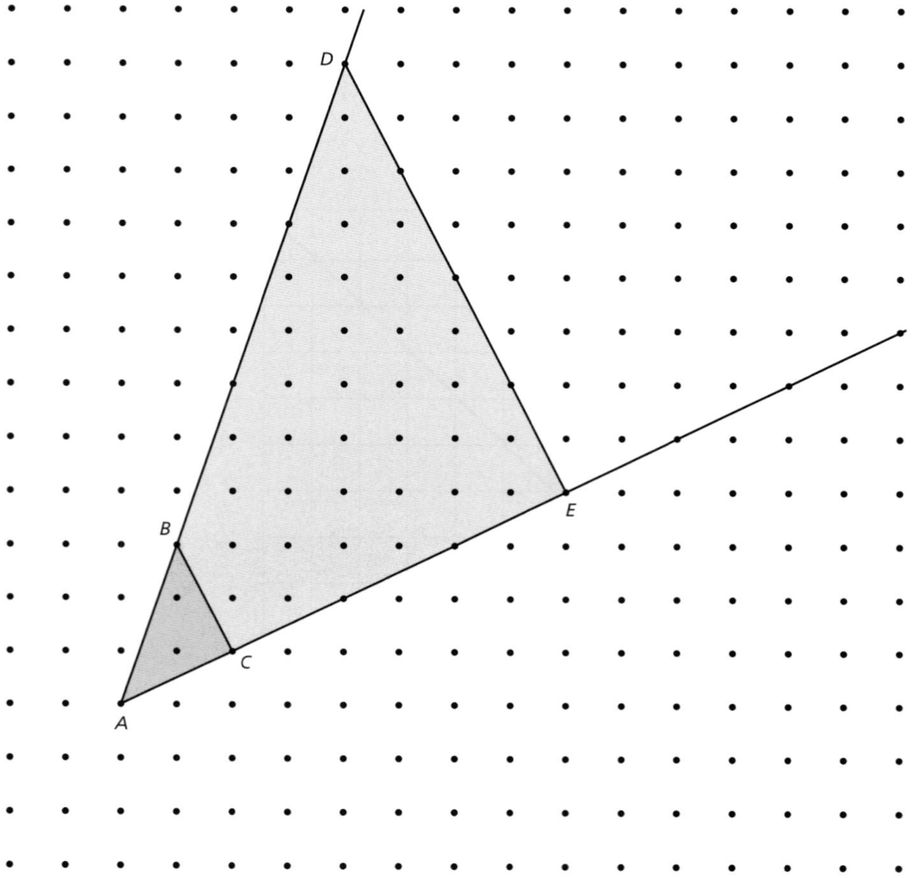

(ii) 40 cm² (2)   **(iii)** 22.4 cm (2)

21 **(i)** (3)

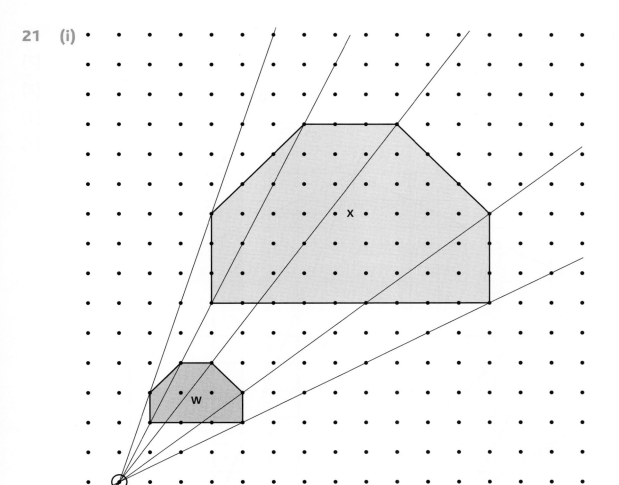

(ii) 5 cm² (2) **(iii)** 45 cm² (2)

22 **(i)** (3)

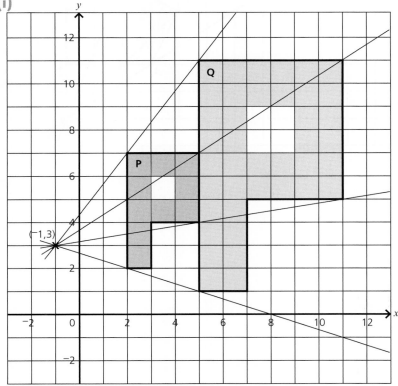

(ii) (a) 10 cm²   (2)

      (b) 40 cm²   (2)

23 (i) 9 cm²   (2)

   (ii) 144 cm²   (2)

  (iii)   (3)

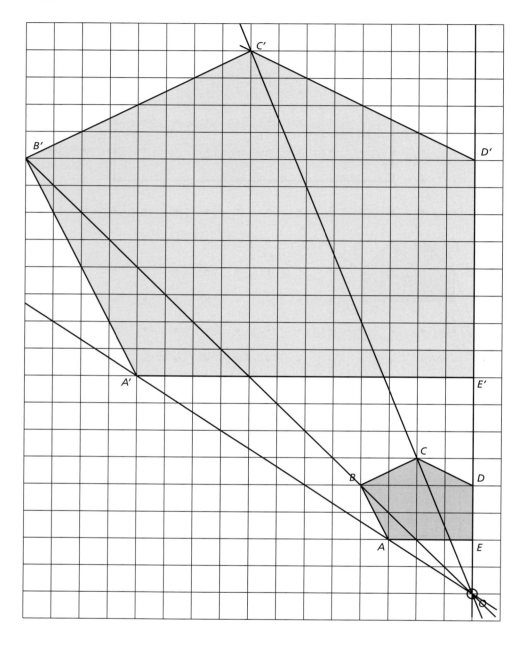

24 **(i)** (3)

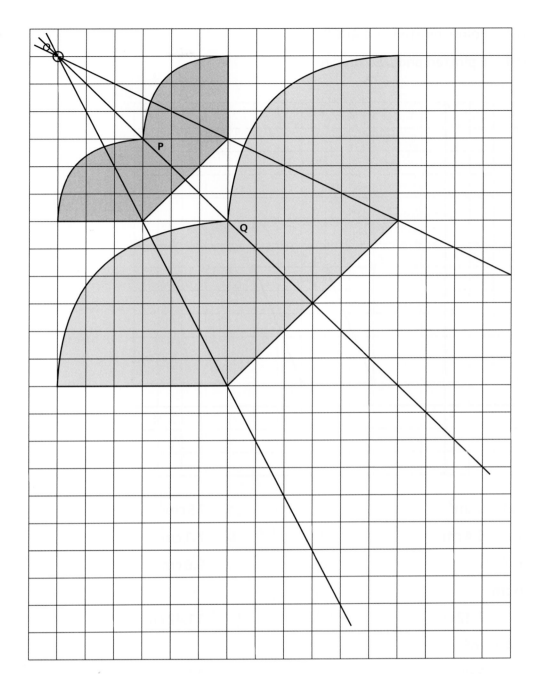

(ii) 18 cm² (3)

(iii) 72 cm² (2)

25 **(i)** **(a)** Points plotted and *ABCD* drawn (3)

(b) *E* plotted and *DEA* drawn (1)

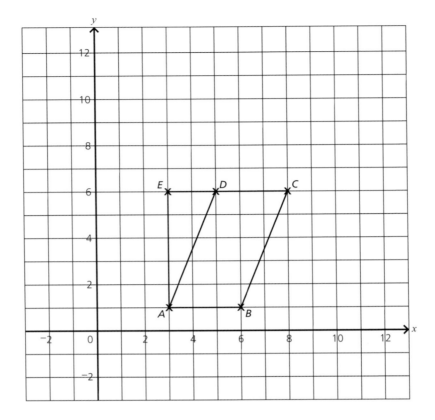

(ii) **(a)** 5 cm² (1) **(b)** 15 cm² (1)

(iii) **(a)** 5.4 cm (2) **(b)** 7.1 cm (2)

26 **(i)** 8.7 cm (2) **(ii)** 9.6 cm (4)

27 **(i)** 6 cm (2)

(ii) **(a)** 7.42 cm (2) **(b)** 11.42 cm (1)

(iii) 34.3 cm² (2)

(iv) **(a)** 22° (3) **(c)** 121° (1)

(b) 44° (2)

28 **(i)** $h = 3.46$ cm (2)

(ii) 6.93 cm² (2)

(iii) 41.6 cm² (2)

(iv) 15.6 cm² (2)

Shape made up of 6 regular hexagons of side 1 cm.

Area of 1 regular hexagon of side 1 cm is $\frac{1}{16}$th the area of a regular hexagon of side 4 cm.

Statistics and probability

→ 6.1 Statistics

1 **(i)** 16 (1) **(ii)** (3)

Number of chips	Tally	Frequency
10–12	IIII	4
13–15	NI I	6
16–18	NI IIII	9
19–21	NI	5
	Total	24

(iii) **(a)** $\frac{7}{12}$ (2) **(b)** $\frac{1}{6}$ (2)

2 **(i)** (3)

Marks	Tally	Frequency
4	I	1
5	II	2
6	NI	5
7	IIII	4
8	II	2
9	II	2
10	II	2
	Total	18

(ii) Range 6 (2)

(iii) **(a)** Mode 6 (1) **(c)** Mean 7 (2)

(b) Median 7 (2)

3 **(i)** (3)

Marks	Tally	Frequency
1	IIII	4
2	NI IIII	9
3	NI I	6
4	NI NI I	11
5	NI NI	10
	Total	40

(ii)

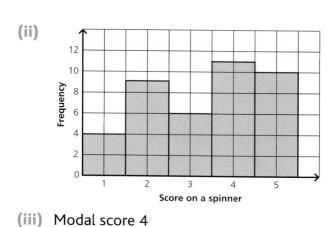

Score on a spinner

(3)

(iii) Modal score 4 (1)

(iv) Median score 4 (2)

(v) Mean score 3.35 (3)

(vi) (a) $\frac{1}{2}$ (1)   **(b)** $\frac{3}{8}$ (1)

4 (i) 20 (2)   **(iv)** 2 (2)

(ii) 50 (2)   **(v)** 2.5 (2)

(iii) 1 (1)

5 (i) (a) 3 (1)   **(c)** 1.5 (2)

(b) 1 (1)

(ii) (a) Giants (2)   **(b)** Huskies (2)

6 (i) 8 (2)   **(ii)** 6 (1)

7 (i) (a) 4.4 seconds (2)   **(c)** 35.16 seconds (2)

(b) 35.15 seconds (2)

(ii) (a) 6.1 m/s (2)   **(b)** 22.0 km/h (2)

8 (i) 7 degrees (1)   **(iii)** 0 °C (2)

(ii) 0 °C (1)   **(iv)** ⁻0.6 °C (2)

9 (i) 4 parsnips (1)   **(ii)** (5)

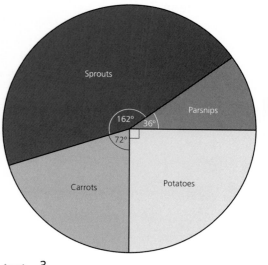

(iii) $\frac{3}{5}$ (3)

10 **(i)** 120° (1)

   (ii) 10° (1)

   (iii) Table completed (3)

Colour of coat	Number of people	Size of angle on pie chart
Blue	12	120°
Red	4	40°
Green	5	50°
Black	8	80°
Yellow	7	70°
Total	36	360°

(iv) 4 (2)   **(v)** Pie chart drawn and labelled (4)

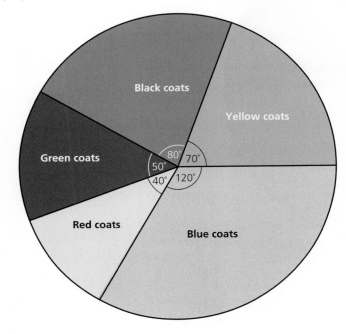

11 **(i)** 15° (2)   **(iii)** $\frac{1}{4}$ (2)

   (ii) 135° (2)

12 **(i)** 20 (1)

   (ii) Table completed (5)

Pop group	Number of children	Size of angle on pie chart
Scream	2	36°
Grubby	3	54°
Sloppydress	9	162°
Gruntalot	6	108°
Total	20	360°

(iii) **(a)** $\frac{3}{20}$ (2)   **(b)** $\frac{11}{20}$ (2)

13 (i) $1\frac{1}{2}°$ (1)   **(ii)** Table completed   (3)

Crop	Size of angle on pie chart
Oil seed rape	225°
Barley	90°
Wheat	45°

(iii) Pie chart drawn and labelled fully   (3)

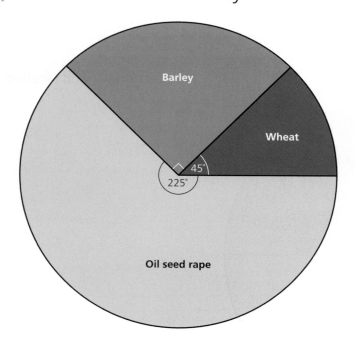

14 (i) (a) 48°   (2)   **(b)** 96°   (1)

(ii) (a) 36 children   (1)   **(b)** 216°   (2)

(iii) 6° represent each child   (2)

(iv)   (2)

Flavour	Number of children	Size of angle on pie chart
Vanilla	8	48°
Strawberry	16	96°
Mint	9	54°
Chocolate	27	162°
Total	60	360°

15 (i) Pie chart drawn with the data recorded below   (5)

Bulb type	Number	Size of angle on pie chart
Daffodils	48	120°
Tulips	18	45°
Crocuses	24	60°
Snowdrops	54	135°

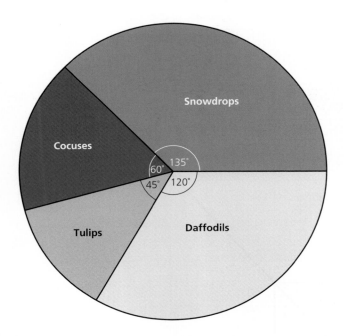

(ii) (a) 37.5% (2)   (b) 30 snowdrops (2)

16 (i) (a) Approximately $69 (2)

(b) £52 (2)

(ii) On flight better value (equivalent to £36) (2)

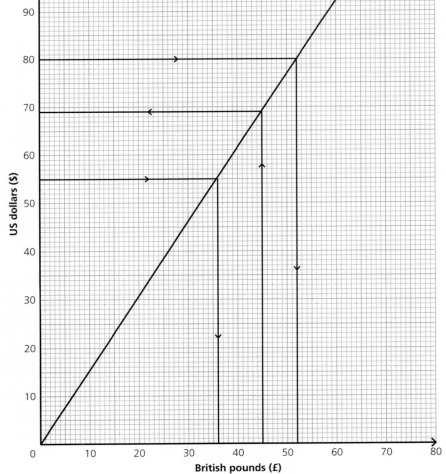

17 **(i)** (2)

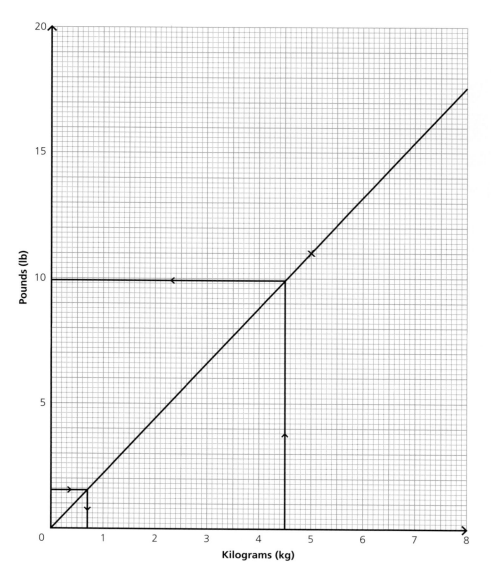

(ii) **(a)** 40 lb (2) **(b)** 700 grams (2)

18 (i)   260 euros   (1)

    (ii)   (4)

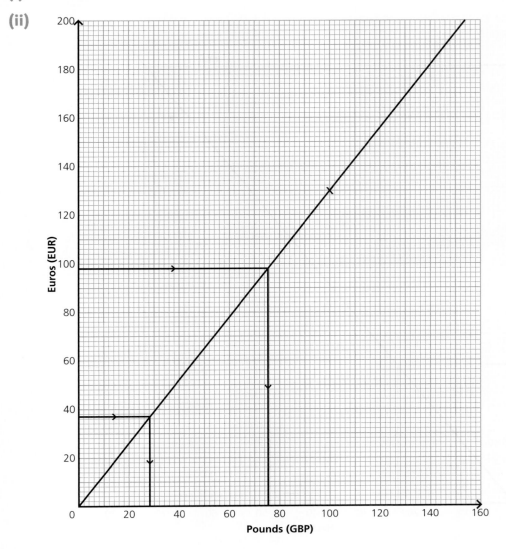

    (iii) £76   (2)   (iv) £28   (2)

19 **(i)** 198 acres (2)

(ii) (3)

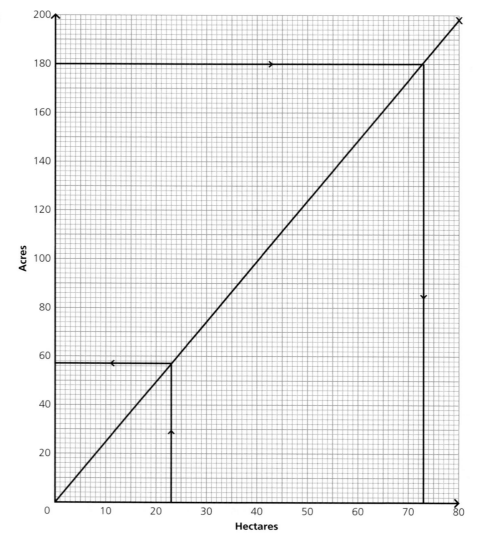

(iii) **(a)** 57 acres (2) **(b)** 73 ha (2)

20 **(i)** £32 (1)

(ii) (2)

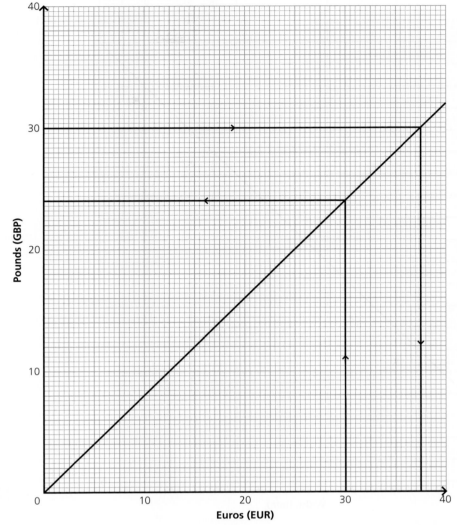

Pounds (GBP)

Euros (EUR)

(iii) **(a)** £24 (2) **(b)** 37.5 euros (2)

21 **(i)**

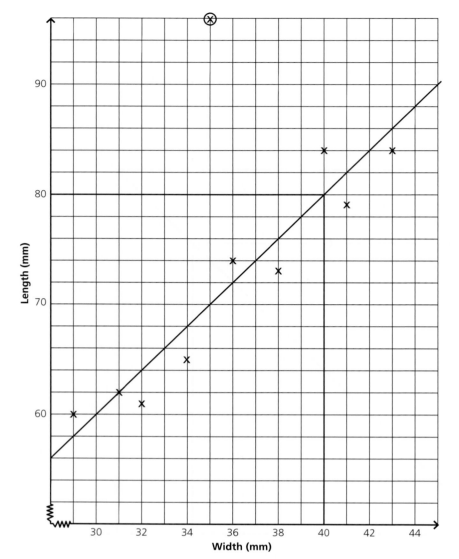

(5)

(ii) Point circled (1)

(iii) Line of best fit drawn (1)

(iv) Positive, fairly high, correlation (1)

(v) 2 : 1

Readings taken vary; examples (30, 60), (40, 80) (2)

22 **(i)** (3)

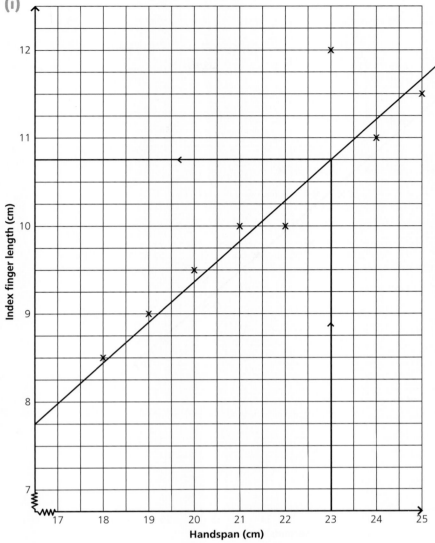

(ii) Line of best fit drawn (1)

(iii) About 10.5–11 cm (2)

23 **(i)** (2)

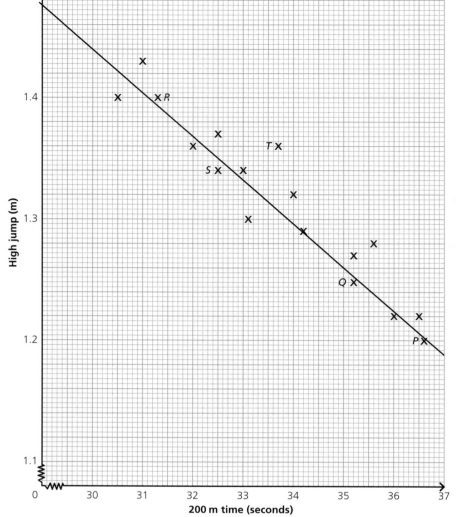

High jump (m)

200 m time (seconds)

(ii) Negative, high, correlation (1)

(iii) A good athlete will record a faster (lower) time and a higher jump (1)

(iv) Line of best fit drawn (1)

(v) About 30.0 seconds (2)

(vi) About 1.28 m (2)

→ **6.2 Probability**

1 **(i)** (2)

H	and	1
H	and	2
H	and	3
H	and	4
H	and	5

T	and	1
T	and	2
T	and	3
T	and	4
T	and	5

(ii) **(a)** $\frac{3}{10}$ (1)   **(b)** $\frac{1}{5}$ (1)

2 **(a)** **(i)** (3)

	H	E	N	R	Y
B	BH	BE	BN	BR	BY
R	RH	RE	RN	RR	RY
I	IH	IE	IN	IR	IY
A	AH	AE	AN	AR	AY
N	NH	NE	NN	NR	NY

   (ii) $\frac{2}{25}$ (2)   **(iii)** $\frac{12}{25}$ (2)

(b) 16 (2)

3 **(i)** (3)

		score on pentagonal spinner				
	×	1	2	3	4	5
score on square spinner	1	1	2	3	4	5
	2	2	4	6	8	10
	3	3	6	9	12	15
	4	4	8	12	16	20

   (ii) **(a)** $\frac{1}{10}$ (2)   **(c)** $\frac{3}{10}$ (1)

   (b) $\frac{3}{10}$ (2)   **(d)** $\frac{3}{10}$ (2)

   (iii) $\frac{7}{20}$ (2)

4 **(i)** $\frac{1}{5}$ (2)   **(ii)** $\frac{19}{25}$ 2)

5 **(i)** **(a)** $\frac{1}{49}$ (1)   **(c)** $\frac{15}{49}$ (3)

   (b) $\frac{24}{49}$ (2)

   (ii) **(a)** $\frac{1}{48}$ (1)   **(b)** $\frac{1}{2}$ (2)

6 **(i)** **(a)** $\frac{1}{6}$ (1)   **(c)** $\frac{1}{2}$ (2)

   (b) $\frac{1}{3}$ (2)

   (ii) **(a)** 20 times (1)   **(b)** 40 times (2)

   (iii) 420 (2)

7 **(i)** **(a)** $\frac{1}{3}$ (2)   **(b)** $\frac{2}{3}$ (2)

   (ii) $\frac{1}{2}$ (1)

   (iii) $\frac{5}{11}$ (2)

8 **(i)** **(a)** $w + g$ (1) **(b)** $w - g$ (2)

(ii) **(a)** $\dfrac{w}{w+g}$ (1) **(b)** $\dfrac{g}{w+g}$ (1)

(iii) $\dfrac{g-1}{w+g-1}$ (2)

9 **(i)** **(a)** $\dfrac{1}{10}$ (1) **(c)** 0 (1)

(b) $\dfrac{1}{5}$ (1)

(ii) **(a)** $\dfrac{1}{9}$ (1) **(c)** $\dfrac{2}{9}$ (2)

(b) $\dfrac{1}{9}$ (1)

(iii) **(a)** $\dfrac{2}{5}$ (2) **(c)** $\dfrac{1}{5}$ (2)

(b) $\dfrac{1}{10}$ (1) **(d)** $\dfrac{3}{10}$ (1)

10 **(i)** **(a)** (2)

	boy	girl
do not like 'hide and seek'	1	2
like 'hide and seek'	3	6

Answers may look different

(b) (2)

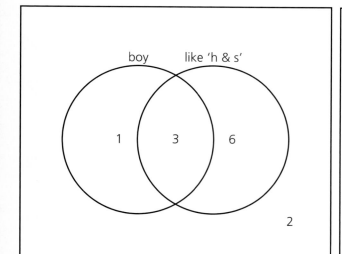 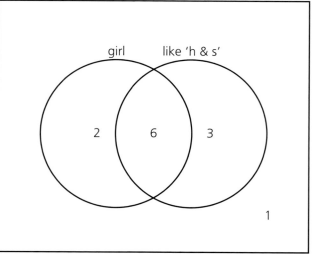

Answers may look different

(ii) **(a)** $\dfrac{1}{4}$ (2) **(b)** $\dfrac{1}{6}$ (2)

11 **(i)** **(a)** A J N O (1)

  (b) A E I J M N S (1)

  (c) B C D F G H K L P Q R T U V W X Y Z (2)

(ii) (4)

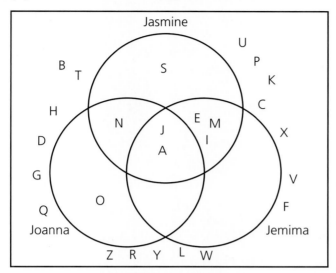

(iii) **(a)** $\frac{9}{13}$ (2)   **(b)** $\frac{3}{13}$ (2)